Her Ladyship's Guide to

Modern

Manners

Her Ladyship's Guide to
Modern Manners

Lucy Gray

BATSFORD

This edition published in 2016 by
Batsford, an imprint of Pavilion Books Group Ltd
1 Gower St
London WC1E 6HD

First published in the United Kingdom in 2005 by National Trust Books

ISBN: 9781849943673

A CIP catalogue record for this book is available from the British Library.

20 19 18 17 16
10 9 8 7 6 5 4 3 2 1

Reproduction by Mission Productions, Hong Kong
Printed by Toppan Leefung Printing Ltd, China

This book can be ordered direct from the publisher at the website:
www.pavilionbooks.com, or try your local bookshop.

Contents

Who needs manners?

That old saying, 'manners maketh Man', has an old-fashioned ring to it – especially in these days of equality. Maybe it conjures up images of upper-crust gentlemen doffing their top hats at one another in the street – rather an anachronism today! But is having good manners really relevant in modern society? Well, of course – good manners are alive and well, and practised by many of us every day of our lives, without even thinking about them much. But sometimes, when we're in situations we're not used to – a formal dinner with lots of silver cutlery, or even a chance to meet the Queen! – we don't know quite how to behave. But don't be nervous – the information in this book will help you to survive in all *manner* of strange situations.

Perhaps we wouldn't describe our behaviour as 'modern manners', but most of us try to abide by accepted rules in our society, and we also notice when those rules are broken or ignored. More and more, we're encouraged to think of ourselves as free spirits, free to do what we please and be true to our own inner nature. But that kind of attitude only works up to a point. Because, in fact, for society to get along smoothly we need to be able to depend on each other, to understand how someone is likely to behave, and to know the best way to respond without making some dreadful *faux pas*. And good manners provide some unwritten ground rules to help us know exactly what type of behaviour we expect in a certain situation. Sometimes it's hard to spot the subtle difference in behaviour, because social behaviour is a very fine-tuned thing. For instance, if you meet a close friend in the street, you'd know that a hug and kiss is a more than acceptable greeting. But if you bump into your boss in the supermarket, you'd probably stop at a friendly hello. A warm hug would cause embarrassment all round. So we need to know what manner to behave in: that's what modern manners are all about.

Good manners can help us get along with all people in society, however different they may appear to be from us. It's natural to notice the difference between people – perhaps their dress, their skin colour or their physical appearance – because of course we're not all the same. But we can treat each other with the same politeness and decency, and the same good manners all round. Our society has changed so much over the last century, and keeps on changing and evolving. Not that long ago, the telephone was a new-fangled device and people worried about what 'etiquette' to use when they spoke down it. Today, more than a few of us have the some worries about what kind of manners to use when writing an email message to a friend or colleague. Modern manners tackle new concerns, because society is constantly moving on, but all of them are to do with how our society operates. So perhaps this is a good point to have a quick look at how our society got to where it is today.

Good manners can help us get along with all people in society, however different they may appear to be from us.

Class versus tribe

Here's a little potted history of how class-conscious Britain became the society it is today – often called the 'classless society', though some would say that still isn't, quite true.

British society up until the period before the Second World War was very class-conscious. The upper classes, or aristocracy, were relatively few in number. But for centuries, they were the people with most power and influence, who got to decide how the country was run – because they were wealthy landowners who, quite literally, owned the country. They lived by their own social 'rules', which were drummed into them from birth, first in the nursery and later in expensive prep and public schools, where they only met other people from the same social class. As an aristocratic person grew up, this learnt behaviour became second nature.

In some ways aristocratic behaviour was quite autocratic – taking action without considering others – but in other ways it was concerned with running society 'properly', in a very paternalistic way. The eldest sons would eventually inherit their father's estate, while their younger brothers would go into the army, the church or the judiciary. Daughters were married off to the sons of other aristocratic families, so as to produce children to preserve the aristocratic lineage. The whole system was self-perpetuating and almost watertight. Outsiders were supposed to 'know their place' and not attempt to put themselves on a level with their betters. This system had been very efficient and had persisted with only minor modifications for hundreds of years. But it was all about to change.

During the 19th century, a middle class of successful tradesmen had begun to grow in wealth and influence. For the first time, factory owners and shopkeepers could become wealthy in their own right, not through inherited riches. When the middle-class merchants began to get rich, they also wanted a share in the power that governed the country. The aristocracy was challenged, and tried to stop the rise of the middle classes in many ways. One small but effective way of trying to keep the middle classes 'in their place' was by adopting complex aristocratic rules governing manners. A middle-class man might be rich but without an aristocratic upbringing, he'd find it hard to grasp the labyrinthine rules that governed upper-class life – having the correct behaviour, or 'etiquette'. Some aristocrats mocked middle-class 'parvenus', who didn't speak with the right 'upper-class' accent, didn't have the right manners and foolishly tried to mix with their 'betters'.

Undeniably, some middle-class people made the mistake of trying to ape gentlemanly behaviour, leading to embarrassing mistakes – like talking about 'serviettes' when an aristocrat would probably say napkins, or saying 'toilets' instead of lavatories. None of that matters today, of course. Silly customs such as crooking the little finger while holding a tea cup were probably middle-class attempts to 'look posh' that didn't come off. One group of people was trying to emulate the learnt behaviour – or manners – of another social class, and couldn't quite get it right.

Lower- or working-class people came further down the social scale. Their role was to work on the estates of the aristocrats, labour in the factories of the middle classes and be domestic servants for both. The many working-class people were poor, ill-educated and exploited, and firmly 'kept in their place' by the classes above them. But, over time, the lack of social opportunity for the working classes led to growing discontent, and slowly a political and social movement began to grow, its object being to overturn the existing system, to establish one that provided the working poor with a fair share of the wealth they helped to create.

After the Second World War, society changed a great deal. Returning servicemen wanted a fair deal from the country they had fought for, and people demanded political change. A Labour government was elected in 1945, the National Health Service was created, grammar schools provided paid-for education for middle-class children: the welfare state came into being. All these measures helped to support the idea of social equality for all. Even though the class society seemed outwardly to be the same as before, subtle changes were afoot. People wanted to 'move up' in life, and indeed it was now possible to change your lot. But still, in the 1950s, many people still felt the way to success in this was to imitate aristocratic behaviour, in accent, dress sense and manners.

The counterculture revolution of the 1960s reacted against those persistent attitudes, and blew them away. Its youthful leaders, some of them barely out of school, were ostensibly rebelling over trivial things like pop music, clothes and hairstyles. But the real revolution was a call to end an archaic social system based on deference and inequality. The United States had a great influence at this time, as it still does today. In Western Europe, America, and many other countries, a younger generation refused to conform to the class system, or to bow to authority just for the sake of it. The 'Swinging Sixties' were a time of liberation, partly a reaction against the postwar years of privation, but also related to more pressing political changes, like civil rights.

Today, in the United Kingdom, the prewar class divisions in society are not so rigid, and some would say they barely exist. Education and the welfare state have given many people opportunities they would not have been allowed in a prewar society.

Manners are no longer anything to do with whether you are rich, had a private education or grew up in a certain social milieu.

The tribal society

How does all this relate to modern manners? Simply this – manners are no longer anything to do with whether you are rich, had a private education or grew up in a certain social milieu. Yes, there are still plenty of rich people around, some of them descendants of the original aristocrats, some of them still owning large country estates, but they no longer have the right to run the country as they once did. And there are probably just as many, if not more, wealthy people who've become rich through entrepreneurship, or running a business – or just by being celebrities (the 'new aristocracy' perhaps?). People are much more likely, in today's world, to define themselves by their work, their interests, or their background than by their social class, and to enjoy socialising with other people who share one of these aspects – or feel free to mix freely with all members of society. Just go into any British pub, and you're like to meet people from all walks of life.

It's still important to feel that you 'fit in' – especially when you're young and perhaps feeling a bit insecure about your place in life. Ever since the Beatles and the Rolling Stones, and before, younger people have defined themselves by their allegiance to a particular type of music – from mods and rockers in the 1960s, to teenyboppers, Goths, punks and heavy-metal music fans – and the clothes and behaviour that go with it. Every young generation finds its own 'tribes'.

But even the more grown-up among us can admit we often feel happier mixing with like-minded people – people that we understand, and feel we know how to behave with. It's natural, perhaps. For many of us, it's still a bit stressful to be in the company of people who have very different lives and interests from our own. Some people might feel nervous and say 'I'm afraid of saying the wrong thing', and what they are really getting at is that they don't know how to behave in this context, and what the social 'rules' are. But the rules really amount to grasping the basics of good manners – they can make you feel far more confident in different social situations and leave you less awkward and embarrassed.

11

But who decides what good manners are?

We all do. The days are long gone when mysterious aristocratic rules on proper etiquette defined every aspect of good behaviour, although some 'rules of etiquette' are certainly based on sensible ideas of respect and politeness. The relics of upper-class etiquette still exist, mostly in ceremonial and special occasions – like the 'rules' that go with the conventional wedding reception ceremony, on how to word invitations, or who can make speeches and when. But manners, and especially the modern manners that can help us today, spring from simpler and more understandable roots – simply the natural human concern most of us have for other people – and the wish to avoid hurting, embarrassing or inconveniencing others unnecessarily. What some would call 'natural politeness', perhaps – a trust that if we behave well to others, then they'll do the same for us.

In addition, there are what some would call 'formal manners', and these are more like the etiquette of old. When we're in an unusual and formal situation, it's very useful to know a bit about what kind of manners would be in order. But even if you find yourself standing next to the Queen of Spain at a Buckingham Palace garden party, simple politeness and friendly conversation are good manners enough. Even so, for those formal occasions that do still require a bit of ceremony, guidance is – nowadays – usually provided in advance. So, don't worry: if you happen to be knighted one day, somebody at the Palace will be sure to send you some hints on how to behave properly! If you find yourself in an awkward formal social situation, remember that most formal rules – like how to address the Queen – are simply the result of habits and custom built up over time, no more than that. These 'rules' are the last vestiges of that strange aristocratic etiquette, designed to keep the middle classes at bay – but today, you can feel free to revolt!

There are few places today where you won't be admitted unless you're wearing a suit and tie. But, on the other hand, knowing the 'expected' attire to wear at an occasion can be helpful, if it makes you feel more at ease if you fit in. It can also be good manners to show that you respect the nature of the situation and have dressed accordingly.

Are rules made to be broken?

In many senses, yes. The formal 'rules' of etiquette are hardly bothered with by most people today, in normal circumstances. Customs like 'always passing the port to the left' are leftovers from aristocratic dining rules. It seems silly to bother if the person on your right would like a glass – or would like something else to drink! But some of the rules of etiquette – that outdated aristocratic system – carry over into good manners. A lot of them are simple common sense.

Before we leave the formal manners defined by etiquette completely, remember that they had an important role (whatever you may think of it): they were there to help bind a certain social group together – in this case the aristocratic class. And it's apparent, just by looking at the many different ways we define ourselves today, just how much human beings like to feel part of a group – for good or ill. Although today we like to think of ourselves as independent-minded individuals, we also like to fit in with the crowd. And we still, even today, make rules to help us do that.

But I don't need these silly rules!

And, to be honest, there's nothing forcing you to use them, either. Sadly (some would say), bad manners are not illegal. And you don't have to go to society weddings, attend formal parties, get your children christened or wear a tie if you don't want to. But what if your best and truest friend decides on a grand wedding, with all the frills and customs – would you go then? We never know what's coming next, and we can find ourselves changing our minds. Sometimes, it's just easiest to follow a few rather silly formal rules in order to make an event or occasion more pleasant for someone who matters to you – and, you know, that's what good manners are all about.

Have some respect!

How many times might you have heard an older person expressing amazement at a youngster's rudeness? Sometimes they're quite justified, but sometimes it's just a case of misinterpretation. It's easy to forget how much society has changed and how informal and liberated it is today – and still is, in comparison to some less-developed countries. The older generation can think back to days, not too long ago in memory, when society was much more formal. Men were always called by just their surname, bosses always 'Mr' this or that (a female boss would have been almost unheard of). But staff lower down the scale – tea ladies, cleaners and janitors – were referred to by their first name, but in a rather patronising way, almost as if they were comparable to children.

Over the years our society has adopted less formal systems of address as the norm, and most workplaces operate on a completely first-name basis. We're no longer deferential and we no longer put our bosses up on a higher social pedestal (much as some might like it!). On the one hand, the informality we use today helps everyone to feel more equal. But on the other hand, it's sometimes difficult to know how to show your respect towards someone. We call Presidents 'Mr' or 'Mrs' and sometimes Prime Ministers too – almost as a relic of how it used to be. But, on the whole, we tend to quite quickly refer to new acquaintances by their first names, sometimes – in the case of email, for instance – before we've even met them.

We no longer treat going to see our doctor, our priest or our children's teachers as formal occasions, though there was a time when people 'dressed up' to go to the doctor, and no woman would leave the house without her hat on. Life has changed, and we regard these people as equals, providing us

There was a time when people 'dressed up' to go to the doctor, and no woman would leave the house without her hat on.

with a service or information and to be valued for their talents and skills. But we can still show natural respect to people, simply through the way we treat them.

And we need to remember too, in such a mobile society as ours, that there are many people who may have come here from a very different social situation in a different country, perhaps one where formality is still more normal. To call them by their first name, especially perhaps someone of an older generation, may make them feel very awkward. Good manners means considering what they are used to, as well.

Indeed, some professions preserve an artificial formality, as a way of keeping a professional distance between people. Somehow it would seem strange if lawyers and judges in the Crown Court referred to each other by their first names, when 'My Learned Counsel' or 'M'Lord' are what everyone expects. Even in ordinary meetings we refer to 'Madam Chair'. And many of us still retain formality when addressing our doctor, or our member of parliament. Forms of address, like other examples of formal manners, or etiquette, often have a helpful purpose – they prevent informality when we *don't* really want it. There are times when we'd rather keep it as professional as possible, because then nobody is going to 'take something personally' when it wasn't intended that way.

Whatever modern manners are, they certainly are not fixed. As society changes, so do manners – because manners reflect the way we act towards each other in our daily lives.

A few basics

Punctuality

Arrivals...

Time is of the essence – and being on time is important, so it gets a whole section to itself. Think about it: being on time for appointments and social occasions is simple good manners, modern or otherwise. Some good advice: for any social occasion, find out when you are expected to be there, and be there on time. Easy! Perhaps that seems obvious to you? Well, that's good. But, if you're always late – or are always left waiting for somebody else who is – see if you recognise any of these types:

First of all there's the 'I just couldn't get my act together' person. Some people are so disorganised that they are always dashing from one appointment to another, late for everything, and always find themselves arriving breathless at the door, apologising profusely. We've all been in that situation sometimes, but if you're always finding yourself saying to your friends, 'Oh, you know what I'm like – I'd be late for my own funeral!', then think about it. Perhaps, like you, your friends think it's just an endearing little fault. Or perhaps they don't – if you've actually made them miss the beginning of the film, or the train they'd planned to catch. Or perhaps you're the friend who always has to wait, and then you'll know how aggravating that kind of behaviour can be.

Then there's the 'I just didn't check the time' person. They arrive very late and, to be honest, don't care when they turn up.

They assume the host will be thrilled to see them, whenever they arrive. They don't think about whether people have been worried about their whereabouts, or whether the other dinner guests have had to sit waiting.

Finally, there's the 'look at me!' attention-grabber, who is well aware that they're late – that's the way they planned it. They want to make a grand entrance and be noticed by everyone in the room. Ideally, they'd like to come down a long flight of Hollywood steps, in a feather boa.

Are you one of those, or do you recognise them? Whichever latecomer you, or the person you're thinking of, may be, being late is, essentially, just being rude. Not good manners at all.

Good manners when it comes to punctuality aren't difficult to acquire. Be on time – it's only considerate, after all. Even the simplest party has taken a bit of an effort, and your hosts are looking forward to

Be on time – it's only considerate, after all.

seeing you. Even if there is a later showing of that film, why should your friend wait outside in the rain for twenty minutes, wondering what happened to you this time. Put yourself in the other person's position, and good manners become an easy matter. And just think – you won't have to make excuses for being late, and they won't have to get stressed out waiting.

What if you're the host of that party – how can you help? Well, always make sure to be quite specific about time when you invite someone, unless you really don't mind when they turn up (and then tell them that). But you can't be too school-marmish about it – it's helpful to allow a bit of leeway, to allow for some guests getting caught in traffic or being unavoidably detained. So, if you say something like 'do come 8 for 8.30' (meaning, we'll eat at 8.30, so come some time before then, but after 8pm) if you want to ensure that people won't be late. And if you're a guest, make sure you allow time for that unexpected eventuality, like a pile-up on the motorway ahead. Things can, and often do, go wrong – so makes sure you plan ahead.

What if you really can't avoid being late?

Sometimes there's nothing you can do about it – if the babysitter didn't turn up, or you got delayed at work, or the trains weren't running. If you can, phone ahead and warn your friend or host that you've been delayed, and why. Let them know what time you expect to be there and apologise briefly. When you do arrive you can make a proper apology but for now keep it short – don't forget they may be looking after their other guests, or waiting in the rain, depending on the situation. Always give the reason why you're unavoidably late – if people have already been waiting half an hour to eat, because you weren't there, they'll at least appreciate knowing why. If you're the host of a dinner party and someone 'calls in late', you should never let your impatience show – even if your guest has no real excuse, and you think they've just been very inconsiderate. It's good manners to rise above it, and not let your annoyance show. Why should your other guests have to deal with your annoyance, or the tension in the air when your guest arrives? Keep the atmosphere pleasant, don't embarrass your guests – save it for after they've gone!

Being late is one thing. The other gaffe you can make is arriving too early. Arriving early at a dinner party or drinks is only acceptable when the hosts are very close friends, and they have let you know they could do with some help getting things set up, or keeping the kids occupied. In other circumstances, being early can be just as inconsiderate as being late, and not good manners at all. Your hosts are probably looking forward to having time to change, and a five-minute breather before the hordes arrive. Don't be the one who spoils their moment of quiet relaxation!

...and departures

When is it time to leave? Many people find it difficult to know just when to go, and either leave too early or outstay their welcome. It's good manners to choose your moment appropriately but also, if you're the host, it's good manners to let your guests know without appearing rude. For instance, if you want an event to finish at a particular time, it's quite in order to make this clear on the invitation. It's not at all unusual to do this when you have booked a public venue, or the event is an 'at home' or, perhaps, in honour of someone who is frail or older, and needs to rest. On the other hand, it can look rather eccentric, and even rude, to tell dinner guests that the evening will finish at a certain time – normally you have to rely on your guests to make their departure tactfully, even though you can drop a few hints (offering coffee for a second time or yawning discreetly sometimes help!).

If you're a guest, choosing the right moment to leave an event can be awkward. You're not alone if you're one of those people who just doesn't know when to say 'I must be getting off now.' If you genuinely have another appointment to go to, make sure you tell your host right at the outset, when they invite you – they won't think you rude if you explain that you'd love to come to lunch, but will have to leave early to get to a previously planned engagement. But they will think you rude if, later on in the evening, you suddenly 'remember' another appointment, as an obvious excuse to get away.

Who's going first? It's always a problem at a party – nobody wants to be first to leave, because it seems as if they're keen to go. Eventually somebody will take the plunge and offer their farewells, and then usually others seize the opportunity to join them. A mass exit of this sort is quite acceptable. If you're the host, don't be offended if some people have to leave early, either – some people need to get back home for various reasons, or may have an early start tomorrow. But, as a guest, whatever time you leave a party, you should seek out the host or hosts, let them know that you're off now, and thank them for their hospitality. One obvious item of tactful good manners: tell them you had a good time, even if you didn't. And however much you long to slip away unnoticed from that really boring party, don't. Apart from the fact that it's just not good manners, you'll probably not get away with it – Fate always steps in at such moments, and your host will probably catch you in the act of sneaking into the coat room and out of the back door. Be polite: it doesn't take long to say goodbye, after all!

But, even if the party is amazingly good, don't outstay your welcome. Unless you've been asked to stay the night, assume that your hosts would quite like you to leave before the cock crows for tomorrow. Judging this is a fine art – it depends on the kind of party, and the kind of hosts. Some friends are quite happy to stay up nearly all night, chatting and enjoying each other's company. In that case it's obviously fine to stay into the wee hours. Other hosts may have small children, or be obviously exhausted. Use your intelligence – if you find yourself in the middle of a long monologue, and your hosts are asleep on the sofa, it's time to go. Actually, it was time to go quite a while back.

If you're a host stuck with a guest who just won't take the hint, it's quite acceptable to stifle a yawn and say 'Oh well, must get to bed now. We've got an early start tomorrow.' Some people need a good dig in the ribs before they'll take the hint and leave – help them out a little.

The truth and nothing but the truth

When is it good manners to tell the truth? And when is it good manners to tell a few white lies? Good manners involve more than a bit of diplomacy – in essence, your considerate good manners help create situations where events turned out as desired, with the least amount of friction. Sometimes a few fibs help that along – it's up to you. It was the young George Washington who said he 'couldn't tell a lie', admitting to his father that he'd cut down the cherry tree – but how many of us could say we are compulsive truth-tellers in that league? Not many. Most people don't want to hear the 'unvarnished truth' about themselves, especially if it's not too pleasant. That's not to say we have to go around flattering everyone and telling them how marvellous and wonderful they are, but it can be good manners to avoid awkward subjects, and tell a little white lie on occasion. If it saves someone's feelings, and does no other harm, there isn't much cost to you – and it will help someone to feel good about themselves, perhaps.

Most people don't want to hear the 'unvarnished truth' about themselves, especially if it's not too pleasant.

Sometimes, however much people ask for it, they don't really want your advice. Beware of being too direct in your opinion, especially if being 'outspoken' may hurt someone. Put yourself in the other person's position and, especially if you have a negative opinion in mind, perhaps keep it to yourself. In general, the only time for a really straightforward opinion is if you have been hired to give professional advice, of a factual nature. However much a friend genuinely appeared to want your opinion, bear in mind that they may not be expecting what you could say – and your friendship could be damaged as a result.

Manners and snobbery

In theory, manners are a way to help us behave in a civilised way towards our fellow members of society. Anyone can have good manners. In our so-called classless society, however, there's still a great deal of snobbery around. And there are still public-school-educated folks with 'cut-glass' accents, and many less privileged members of society – some of whom may have accents that others deem 'common' or 'working-class'. These distinctions are hard to eradicate, and are often ingrained. Good manners involve rising above such snobby behaviour as calling those you deem less cultured than you 'oiks' or 'chavs', for instance, or – on the other hand – reverse snobbery, such as calling the landed gentry 'hooray henrys' or 'public-school twits'. Perhaps it's human nature to feel more comfortable among those who share our own values, but that doesn't mean that we have to avoid the company of people from other parts of society, and doesn't give us, or them, any right to feel superior. Eleanor Roosevelt once said: 'No one can make you feel inferior without your consent.' She was, as so often, very wise. If you are confident of who you are and what you are worth, you will be able to walk with kings. You don't have to treat people from other walks of life as enemies to be guarded against. You merely have to show them that you are quite comfortable in your own skin and that you assume the same respect from them that you give to others.

Not in front of the children

Unless you choose to join an enclosed religious order, you're going to meet children in a variety of social situations. If you're invited to a social occasion, it's only good manners to ask your host if your children are welcome, and to understand if the host indicates that it's not really an occasion where children would be happy. Listen carefully to your host's answer and judge for yourself whether they mean children are really welcome or that they are merely tolerated. Don't take offence if it seems that, on this occasion, it's really an adult affair – some events, like a formal dinner party for instance, just aren't suitable for kids, who'll probably be bored and tired anyway, and may spoil it for everyone else, including you. You may be used to your kids creating mayhem, running around playing and generally doing what children do. But, if it's not a family *There are plenty of* event, your hosts – and the other *kids who can be relied* guests – may find this rather *upon to enjoy a grown-* distracting. Yet your children are of *up party and even to* course part of the family, and you may *help by refilling glasses* want them to come along – especially *and taking round* if you know they are capable of *plates of food.* behaving politely and not being disruptive to others. There are plenty of kids who can be relied upon to enjoy a grown-up party and even to help by refilling glasses and taking round plates of food. Bear in mind that you might have to bribe them with some extra pocket money though!

If you are the host you have a couple of options when it comes to inviting guests with kids. A good one, if you have the stamina, is to throw an extended party in which Part One takes place in the afternoon or early evening and is for families with kids and Part

Two is held later and is for adults only. Alternatively, you can go out of your way to have a children's room and provide toys, games, videos or whatever to keep the children happy. This can work well but it does mean that adults will have to keep an eye on the proceedings.

Both parents and hosts should bear in mind that kids don't necessarily all want to play together – especially if they have never met before. Don't force your kids to 'join in' with all the games and other children's activities: if they're happiest reading a book in the corner, or staying with you, let them. Our considerate good manners need to extend to the kids as well!

At some of the more formal occasions, like weddings, children can become a bit overwhelmed, especially tiny children and babies, who might start crying at just the wrong moment. Although everyone loves to see that tiny bridesmaid, or the adorable little pageboy, it's good manners to make sure there's an adult nearby who'll take charge if the occasion becomes too much, and bawling commences. A hug and a kiss is often all it takes, and can do a lot to keep the day special and happy for everyone.

In the same way, it's important to consider other people in public places, such as restaurants, where wandering or wailing kids can really spoil other people's enjoyment. Even though you might be longing just to relax and enjoy your meal, it's good manners to think about the other diners. Don't let small children run around bothering people who may find them a bit of a nuisance, and don't take offence if other people don't seem thrilled to be surrounded by small toddlers. Children are children, of course. But they're also quite capable of sitting and enjoying their meal without too much hyperactivity – and it's the way to learn the good manners that you'll be teaching them by example. But you can only do your best, and most fellow diners in a family restaurant will probably sympathise – they've almost certainly been in the same boat.

One tricky question is whether children should attend family funerals. In the old days the answer was 'of course', then received wisdom swung the other way and at one point it was deemed quite inappropriate. Now the pendulum has swung back quite a long way and the feeling seems to be that, as long as the children understand what's going on, they should be allowed to say goodbye with everyone else. It is a decision that should be based on the maturity of the child, and whether or not they want to attend.

Another difficult issue is that of children and medical treatment. Attitudes have changed a lot and now by the time the children reach secondary school it is likely that they will be treated as responsible people able to speak for themselves. While they are pre-teens you will still be welcome to attend the consultation, but as they get a bit older you may find it suggested that they should see the doctor alone. They can even go to get medical advice and treatment without your knowledge and consent. Many parents find this deeply troubling. They feel that their role is being undermined by outsiders. But if you ensure that your relationship with your kids is close enough that they feel they can confide in you, they are likely to tell you about any medical problems that concern them, or even ask for you to accompany them to see their doctor.

Sorry seems to be the hardest word

We all end up in situations where an apology is necessary. Sometimes it's simply making a tactless remark, or putting our foot in it. Or perhaps we lost our temper for a moment and snapped at someone – friend or family – or did or said something we now regret. None of us are perfect, and all of us have the ability to say 'sorry', and mean it.

Saying 'sorry', and meaning it, is not a sign of weakness. Far from it. It's a sign of good manners and consideration. That mythical person who said, 'Never apologise and never explain', was trying to sound tough, but succeeded only in being insensitive, and really rather crass. What on earth is wrong with trying to make amends if we have done something thoughtless or hurtful?

Saying 'sorry', and meaning it, is not a sign of weakness.

How to say sorry depends on the nature of the apology, and what it's for. Barging into someone in the street because you weren't looking where you were going can usually be put it right with a simple, 'I'm so sorry, I didn't see you', and a big, apologetic smile. If the apology is for something a bit more 'serious', you'll need to say sorry in the most appropriate way. For example, if you said something hurtful or did something thoughtless that offended a friend, then a quick, 'Whoops, sorry!' just won't do the trick. They may think you're mocking them, and are unlikely to believe your apology. Sometimes a little present can go a long way to helping an apology along, but don't think you can necessarily buy your way to forgiveness. Above all, you need to talk with the person you inadvertently offended, and try hard to put matters right. You can't rush this sort of thing and it's no good hoping that just saying the right words will get you off the hook. You have to mean them, too.

Not all apologies are of the personal variety. If you mess up at work – perhaps forgetting to deliver something with an important deadline, or losing a vital file – the only thing you can do is 'own up' and say sorry. Don't try to conceal the problem, because people are bound to find out eventually and will respect you far less if you didn't come clean in the first place. Usually a problem can be solved and the quicker the better – explain what went wrong, say sorry, help to rectify the situation if you can. Just remember how little we respect some of those particularly evasive politicians who try to avoid answering difficult questions, or are insincere in their responses. Don't be like them – your manners are better than that!

One situation in when it pays to stop and think before you say 'sorry' is when a formal letter is required or a legal situation is implied. Then it's best not to say 'sorry, my fault' straight away, even if you want to help smooth things out. If you and another driver have a prang at a crossroads, don't leap out of your car and immediately start offering profuse apologies. It may not have actually been your fault, even if you are trying to be nice! In this case you want to keep things formal, so that you can go through the proper insurance procedures. Exchange details, ask any witnesses for their name and contact number, and check that everyone is okay. But hire a lawyer if apologies are required.

Finally, sometimes we are in the position of having to apologise for something that was not our own fault. If someone has taken offence at something for no reason you can see, or if someone blames you for something that was, by rights, caused by a colleague's action, what can you do? Where the problem is trivial, often the simplest, and most well-mannered route is to quietly apologise to defuse the situation.

Oh, don't mention it...

Receiving an apology can be almost as difficult as offering one. Good manners call for you to be gracious when someone makes you a heartfelt apology. Rubbing someone's nose in their mistake will make you look petty-minded and vindictive. Just as the apology needs to be sincere, so does the acceptance. It is pointless to say that you forgive someone if you don't, but you can still be civil in your response, and listen to what the person has to say. If the apology is personal, it is important that the person understands how hurt you were – but don't go on and on about it: just say your piece, and stop. Don't use an incident to gain some kind of emotional sway over a friend and never bear grudges.

If someone has made a mistake, remember that nobody's perfect, and everyone makes errors or tactless remarks sometimes. We are all human and fallible and every now and then everyone manages to drop a really heavy brick. That can hurt, but if someone has the decency to explain and apologise sincerely you ought to accept. But on the other hand, of course you're under no obligation at all to let someone off if they are just anxious to get out of an awkward situation or if they make a habit of being thoughtless. With friends like that, who needs enemies? And it might be time to cool it towards that particularly thoughtless person.

Saying 'sorry' almost seems to be an unconscious 'tic' for many Brits, and quite a few foreigners get rather confused by the amusing British habit of apologising for things that are not their fault. When an American asks, 'Is this the train for Kings Cross?' we reply, 'No, sorry, this one goes to Kings Lynn.' Why on earth are we sorry, they wonder? We didn't make the mistake and we've just saved someone from a long journey in the wrong direction. So, perhaps it's best to concentrate hard on not saying sorry unless you've actually done something wrong!

The golden rule

Is there anything more important than fitting in with the crowd? Although people have many different ideas about how to behave and some of these ideas may be contradictory, there is a general consensus among most people that kindness and consideration for others are basic values to which we all must aspire. No matter what else you may get wrong, as long as you stick to these two things you will never be far wrong and it's unlikely that you will ever get into a situation that cannot be salvaged. Your considerate good manners will see you through. In fact your consistent respect and thoughtfulness will probably mark you out to others as someone deemed to have 'natural politeness' and 'a good nature'. And, even if you've put a lot of work into your manners, you should take that as one of the highest compliments going!

Party people

We're all social animals, aren't we? Some of us are more outgoing than others but, on the whole, few people object to a good party with friends. What's more, we need to meet and interact with people – often a wide variety of people in different social and work-related situations. All these social events help to 'oil the wheels' of the society we live in. So we meet in all sorts of ways – parties, conferences, business meetings, cultural events and nights out with our friends – and we can be very inventive in our reasons for getting together. 'Let's get together for a drink!', 'Come over and we'll play a round of golf with Jack and Mary', 'We should hook up to go to a play together some time', 'Fancy a coffee next Saturday?'. And when we meet up, we get on with all sorts of social activities, depending on the situation. We may make friends, do business, plot and plan, select new sexual partners, exchange gossip and just strengthen the bonds that hold our various social 'tribes' together. For most of us, socialising is both a pleasure and a necessity and knowing how to behave makes every event easier and more effective. Having a good grasp of the modern manners suitable for a variety of different social occasions will help them to go well for you, and what manners to use depend slightly on the social occasion.

Invitations

How do you send them, and how do you respond to them? Today, an invite can be as formal as a gold-edged card covered in fancy copperplate writing, or merely a hastily scrawled note, a text message or a quick message on the answerphone. Really there are no strict rules on what form an invitation should take, although it's unlikely that your invitation to attend that Buckingham Palace garden party will arrive by fax. The more formal the occasion, the more formal the invitation is likely to be.

Send...

If you're not the sort to give big formal parties all the time, deciding what sort of invitation to send, and what it should say, can be a bit daunting. But don't worry – you can get a lot of help on this. If you go along to your local printer or copy shop, you'll find they have all kinds of samples you can look at, as well as suggested wordings. You can even look for samples on the Internet, and order them that way. The simplest advice is that you should keep your wording clear and concise, with details of time, place and, if it matters, dress code. Make sure you explain clearly what kind of event it is – a wedding or baby-naming ceremony, or an 18th birthday, or whatever. If it's a formal occasion, it's probably best not to try to be funny or too 'original', as people may misunderstand. You may want people to RSVP – so that you can get a good idea of how many people to expect. Incidentally, the letters RSVP at the bottom of an invitation stand for *Répondez s'il vous plaît* (meaning 'Answer, please'), and are a leftover from the days of aristocratic etiquette, when French was the most fashionable language. If you put RSVP on the invitation, you must provide an address, or perhaps just a phone number or email address, which people can reply to.

...and receive

When you receive an invitation the most important rule of all is that you must reply, and promptly – not at the last minute, even if you don't intend to go. And even if there is no 'RSVP' on the bottom of the invitation, you really should let people know whether you are able to attend, if there is a way. Think about how difficult it is to cater an event if you're not sure how many people to expect, or when – it's good manners to help lower your host's stress levels if you can! Also, if you have said you will be coming and then find that something has come up that you just can't get out of, it's good manners to call your hosts and send your apologies, as soon as you can.

Replying to an informal invitation is easy – usually you can just phone or email. For formal invitations, it's more usual to reply in writing, and to write in the third person. So, if you get an ornate wedding invitation that says something like 'Mr and Mrs John Smith invite you to the wedding of their daughter Julie to Mr Alan Jones', you'd probably write back 'Mrs Jane Evans thanks you for your kind invitation and will be delighted to attend.' And remember to write back to the person who sent the invitation – in this case Mr and Mrs John Smith, rather than the people who are actually getting married. But, actually, even formal occasions are getting more and more flexible in the way they invite people, so don't be surprise or put off if the invitation indicates that a phone call would be acceptable. And, similarly, when many people are hosting their own marriages or other formal get-togethers, they are likely to send out the invitation in their own name, rather than Mum and Dads'.

Playing host

There's an art to being a good host. Some would say that if you're enjoying your own party, then you can't be doing a good job as host. That's not necessarily true, but perhaps what they're getting at is that you have to do a lot of work to make a party go well. You need to be seeing to your guests, making sure they have refreshments, introducing them to people they might like to meet and, just as important, keeping them away from people that might rub them up the wrong way.

If the party is an informal 'walk about' (or even dance about!), your job as host is to keep circulating, because it's your job to make sure that people are happy and interested and not feeling unwanted. Remember that you're probably the only person in the room who knows a bit about every guest present, so you can introduce people to each other and start the conversation between them. Try and find something they might have in common, or something unusual or interesting that might start them chatting. But don't reveal personal secrets or embarrassing information! 'Jack, you must meet Bob – he's got the most wonderful house, quite near where you used to live' is fine. 'Jill, you must meet Joan – she's in therapy for depression too' is probably not! Once you've got a conversation started, move on after a few minutes. Don't monopolise people and don't let them monopolise you. Your job is to make everyone feel wanted. If you see someone who is clearly feeling a bit left out you need to introduce them to someone they might get on with. If you see cliques forming you should try to break them up as tactfully as possible. The sort of party where all your friends from the office, for example, take over one room and chat to each other while freezing out any interlopers is to be avoided at all costs. It helps if you have activities that get people talking to each other. If it's a fun event, like a Christmas party, you can even have some silly games.

It helps if you have activities that get people talking to each other.

At formal professional or work gatherings, such as conferences or business parties, it can be helpful to give people name badges.

This saves everyone the trouble of having to ask names and then perhaps mishearing them or forgetting them and then having to bluff their way through the rest of the event. If it's a professional meeting, you can also include the person's job or company, which helps to provide a conversation opener, so guests can approach each other. Remember that your job as host is to make everything as easy and comfortable as possible for your guests. Anything that might cause a guest difficulty or embarrassment should be dealt with swiftly and smoothly. Little things like where to park the car and where they can safely leave coats can cause guests a problem right at the beginning of an event, so make sure you have that sorted out already. And during the party, small embarrassments – like a dropped glass of wine – should be cleared up quickly with a smile and a quick 'don't worry about it!' A good host thinks ahead, to put their guests at ease.

Some people just love throwing parties. Others don't. That's fine: if you don't feel up to being an extrovert and capable host, then consider hiring staff to help you out, especially for a larger, formal do. You can also hire caterers to do all the cooking, serving – and the washing up. And why not – it may cost a bit, but many people think that it's money well spent, especially for a once-in-a-lifetime party. Today it's not just big wedding receptions that have caterers: some people hire a caterer to provide the food for the small dinner party at home, or for an informal birthday bash.

And while we're on the subject of food and drink: do always make sure that everyone has enough. But also, as host, don't force food and drink on people, even if you can't understand why they wouldn't want more. And lastly, if alcohol is being served, watch out for people who may have had 'one too many'. Try to make sure they stop drinking if you can – quietly removing their glass or the bottle can be more polite, and effective, than getting cross –

and certainly don't let them drink or drive. Offer to call them a taxi, arrange for them to be dropped off by a sober guest who's going the same way – even offer them a bed for the night, if that's the only option.

Safety first

Your final duty as a good, well-mannered host is to make sure that everyone gets home safely, as much as you can. Make sure that younger and older guests, especially, have a lift home. Know which guests you can trust to take people to their front door. It's simple common sense, but can do a lot to make your guests leave feeling happy.

How to be a great guest

You may feel that being a great guest just involves turning up and enjoying yourself. Actually, that's not strictly true. First of all, for most private parties it's good manners to bring a small present for your hosts. Safe, if rather uninspired, choices are a bottle of wine, a bunch of flowers or perhaps a small flowering plant or a box of chocs. That's more than acceptable for most situations. If you know your host very well and have an idea of their taste, you could bring something a bit more adventurous – a rose bush for that gardening-fanatic friend, or some scented candles that match your friend's newly decorated bathroom. But keep to safe choices unless you know your hosts well.

Once you've arrived, it's good manners to think about the other guests. If most guests know each other, look out for any newcomers who may feel a bit left out. Make a point of chatting with them and helping the social situation along. If conversations are getting a bit 'cliquey', try to steer them to more general areas where everyone can join in. There's nothing more bad-mannered than a group of guests who stand around gossiping and making in-jokes that the other guests can't understand. Help your host out by making sure all guests are involved in the social interaction.

If the food is a buffet or other informal situation and there are no professional waiting staff, you can help a bit by handing round snacks to the guests near you, or keeping glasses topped up. You don't need to spend the whole time doing these things but it is polite to lend a hand when it is needed. And actually, if you are yourself feeling a bit shy or awkward, it can be a good way of keeping yourself occupied and being 'part of things'.

At the end of the evening, if you're driving, you might ask if anyone is going your way that needs a lift. You may save a grateful person a taxi fare and also have some company on the way home. If you need a lift yourself, it's quite in order to ask if anyone's going your way, or to ask your host if you might phone for a taxi.

Some people like to send their host a note thanking them for the party and telling them how much they enjoyed it. This custom is becoming rare these days but it is a nice one. It is always touching to receive a little thank-you card, or even an email or text message. All you need to say is how much you enjoyed the evening and add some pleasantries about the food or the company. Two or three sentences at most will do the job.

Meeting and greeting

What are the rules when it comes to introducing yourself to strangers at a social event? It can be awkward to find yourself in a situation where you don't know anyone, or would like to make yourself known to someone, but there is no host around to do the introductions. But things have changed. It used to be the case that rules for introductions were strictly observed as part of social etiquette. Men had to be introduced to ladies, and young people were introduced to their elders. People were very formal and addressed each other in ways befitting their status in society. None of that now applies, you'll be very glad to hear, but that doesn't mean that there are no longer any rules. There are unspoken 'rules', but they are different and less clearly defined. In order to play the social game these days you have to employ some common sense and a little psychology. If you spot someone you'd like to talk to there is nothing wrong with going up to them and introducing yourself. You don't have to be clever, or word your introduction in a particular way. You can just say something basic like 'Hi, I'm Tom, I don't believe we've met,' while holding out your hand to shake. The other person will most likely introduce themselves then, but if not you can say something like 'and you're…?' to encourage them to do so. Remember to smile and use a friendly tone of voice. 'Clever' introductions and smart chat-up lines usually make you look like an idiot. If you don't feel confident enough to go straight up to someone, you can attach yourself to the group they are in and take an opportunity to contribute to the conversation when a gap arises. Sometimes this is hard though, especially if you're a bit shy, or all the other people are deep in conversation. It's often better to seek out the host, and ask them to introduce you to the person you'd like to meet. This way you stand to get a bit of background information about them in advance, which will help ease you into a conversation.

Shaking hands may seem a bit formal to some people, but

In order to play the social game these days you have to employ some common sense and a little psychology when you meet someone for the first time, it's quite in order – whether it's a business or personal social situation. You don't have to do more than give a firm, friendly handshake. Quite brief – no need to pump someone's arm up and down enthusiastically! It goes without saying that you should have clean hands – that may sound pretty obvious, but at a buffet lunch you could find yourself inadvertently covered in salad dressing, so wipe your hands on a napkin first. It's actually quite acceptable, if you are busy balancing a glass and plate of food, to say 'Nice to meet you,

The days are long gone when only men could initiate a handshake, by the way.

Eye contact

In Western culture eye contact, and how we use it, is extremely important in social interaction (things are different in some other cultures). In British society we tend not to look 'straight on' at someone too much until we know them well, although we do make eye contact quite a bit. In North America it's much more normal to make and keep eye contact with anyone you are talking to – so don't be put off if an American seems to be staring at you hard while you converse. In general it's not only good manners but good psychology to look at people while you speak to them. People really will trust you if you give them a lot of eye contact. In fact, you'll often notice that salesmen and woman may look straight into your eyes all the time you're talking with them. They've been trained to convey sincerity (even if some of them aren't sincere!).

I'm afraid my hands are full at the moment,' or something similarly friendly and cheery, if it's impossible to put things down.

If somebody doesn't initiate the handshake, remember that you can. Hold out your hand in a friendly way towards the other person and say 'Pleased to meet you!'. The days are long gone when only men could initiate a handshake, by the way.

The art of conversation

Unless you're a natural chatterer, happy to talk about anything and everything, making conversation at social events can be a bit awkward. What should you talk about, and how? There used to be an unwritten rule that sex, politics and religion were subjects to avoid, except with good friends. But nowadays it's quite all right to talk about these topics in serious conversations with people you've just met. Many people enjoy the cut and thrust of an intellectual or political debate, or like to debate an issue of the day. If you do too, make sure that your companions are genuinely interested in this kind of 'heavy-duty' conversation before you wade in. You wouldn't want them to feel you were directly attacking their beliefs or views and inadvertently get involved in a full-on row. Good manners call for tact and diplomacy and even if someone starts spouting off about something in a way you find quite disagreeable or, in your opinion, wrong, try to react calmly and with restraint. Other people will respect you for it.

Social chitchat, or 'small talk', about day-to-day subjects is usually best unless you are sure you've read the situation correctly. Usually you're well advised to spend a few minutes of conversation with a new acquaintance generally getting to know them and exploring what views and values you may have in common, without getting in too deep. If you end up talking with another guest who, it quickly becomes clear, holds views that are so different from yours you just can't bear to continue the conversation, choose a pause to make an excuse to leave – to get yourself another drink, or go to the cloakroom, for instance. When you come back, find somebody else to converse with. Above all, be gracious about any differences of opinion, and keep the atmosphere civil – you may have to accept that not everyone shares your opinion on certain matters, and also accept that you owe it to your host, as a well-mannered guest, to treat everyone there with respect.

Joking apart

Humour and laughter can help any social conversation to run smoothly, but have to be used skilfully. Don't start telling a joke unless you know that you're good at it – it's very embarrassing to find that you've forgotten the essential punchline. But humour can be useful to get a serious point across in a light way – just don't overdo it. Teasing can be a good way of gently disagreeing with someone you know, but don't tease someone who obviously can't take it. Never tease someone you don't know at all – you may find you've caused deep and permanent offence, but they're just too polite to show it.

Quite a few people are actually very offended by dirty jokes or 'lavatorial' humour, and will be shocked or seriously offended.

Rude or 'dirty' jokes are also a no-go area in the vast majority of social situations. Think twice (or more) before telling any dirty jokes in public, however funny you find them – and however funny other people might too. Quite a few people are actually very offended by dirty jokes or 'lavatorial' humour, and will be shocked or seriously offended. They won't think much of you and you're unlikely to be able to change their opinion. Only use the more 'earthy' jokes in your

41

repertoire when you are absolutely sure that everyone present is likely to share your sense of humour. Never, ever tell sexist or racist jokes: they're not only inexcusable, they are also very likely to cause great offence.

We Brits have a tradition of dealing with difficult situations by making a joke of them. Sometimes those jokes are in appallingly bad taste. It's a kind of coping strategy that most people brought up in Britain have probably encountered. But it's not something that should be tried out on people you don't know well, and certainly not on people from another culture. Although your friends may know that usually you're a caring, sensitive type, the strangers you've been chatting with will only know you as the person telling all those tacky jokes. They may not give you the benefit of the doubt.

There are a couple of things that are real 'no-no's in social conversation. One is using the occasion to ask for some free advice from a professional. Don't sidle up to a guest who happens to be a doctor and ask him how to deal with your piles, or worse. Don't corner the local builder and ask him all about building an extension to your house. When people are at a party they are, most definitely, 'off-duty'. Of course they may chat about their work, often to tell you funny stories about things that have happened there, but they don't want to put on their professional hat, especially to give unpaid advice. If you seriously do want their advice, you can ask for a business card, or ask if you can phone later in the week to make an appointment.

The other thing that you really mustn't do is be a bore. That's a tough one to watch out for because, unfortunately, most boring conversationalists tend not to be the ones who notice they're boring! If you're considerate of others, you're hardly likely to fall into this category. But do make sure that you don't talk compulsively and at length about your work, or insist on telling a stream of stories without letting anyone get a word in. If you haven't heard anyone else talking for a minute or two, or haven't asked anyone a question, consider the possibility that you might have been talking too much yourself. Some people start talking compulsively when they are feeling shy and nervous, but there's nothing wrong with listening for a while. And do remember to change the subject occasionally.

If you really can't think of anything to say, or any subject to talk about, just ask a few interested questions of the person you are with. Most people enjoy being asked about their lives – it can be quite flattering. What do they do for a living? Have they got children, pets, hobbies? How long have they lived in the area? How do they know the host? Listen hard to their responses and you'll almost certainly find some information that you can respond to, or use to ask a follow-up question. 'Ah, you live in Markham Road – I used to live there when I taught at the school. Do they still have that wonderful park at the corner?' Avoid simple yes or no answers to any questions you are asked, as well. It's good manners, however nervous – or even bored – you may be feeling to help out the conversation by offering as much as you can.

Usually you can easily 'feel' your way around a conversation with a new acquaintance at a party or other event. If you have a lot in common and 'get on like a house on fire', you'll know quite quickly. In those circumstances, you may quickly get into quite a chatty and detailed conversation, telling each other about your lives. Other people find it very interesting to chat to people whose lives are very different from their own, even if they are similar in other ways. If you are getting on well with someone, it is quite okay to offer to exchange phone numbers or email addresses.

Body language

Psychologists tell us that human communication is 20 per cent verbal and 80 per cent non-verbal, so if you want to know whether you have clicked with someone, take a look at their body language and be aware of your own. In a social situation you can use body language to convey a positive impression – maintain eye contact with the speaker and stand squarely without fidgeting too much. Turn towards people while they are talking and smile when appropriate, to show you are interested in them. If you adopt a physical bearing that appears confident, you'll be surprised how confident you will actually begin to feel. On the other hand, if you stand in the corner slouching over your glass, or sit hunched up with your arms curled around you – well, you'll be very unapproachable and people will find it hard to know how to talk to you. We all feel nervous at parties sometimes, but we can help ourselves out a lot with careful body language.

If you adopt a physical bearing that appears confident, you'll be surprised how confident you will actually begin to feel.

There are lots of theories about how our body language can indicate what we are really thinking. If someone scratches their nose, or pulls at their ear, it can – some say – indicate that they disagree with the speaker. Of course, they may just have an itch! But we all know that someone whose eyes wander while we're talking to them is not really interested in what we are saying, or that someone who backs away from us is trying to get away from our 'personal space'. At crowded parties, it's sometimes hard to maintain your personal space, or to avoid getting too physically close to other people. Bear in mind that some people may be very nervous if you seem to be crowding them, and even interpret it as a sexual 'come-on'. Unless you meant it that way – and even if you did – do be considerate of how other people may feel. If you get a clear indication that the person doesn't appreciate your closeness and is not interested in that kind of interaction, politely move out of their personal space and chat from more of a distance.

The office party

Ah, the office party – there are few social occasions quite like it, and quite so fraught with peril! Actually there are several kinds.

Office party Type One is the party to which clients and suppliers are invited. This isn't really a 'let your hair down' occasion, but a civilised get-together to thank outside people for their contribution to the firm. These kinds of occasions can be very friendly and chatty, but probably not too informal – after all, these are your customers.

Office party Type Two is the kind often thrown by larger organisations such as banks or corporate businesses. These kinds of parties can be intimidating – you don't want to get drunk and make a fool of yourself in front of your boss, or the people you are boss of. So keep it polite and friendly, and don't overindulge. It's good manners to talk to people in a friendly manner, but don't get too personal or opinionated unless you know your colleagues well.

Some people use big corporate parties as a chance to try and get ahead. It's entirely up to you – if you feel you'd be confident going up to the top brass and introducing yourself, now's your chance. But judge the occasion carefully and make sure that your approach would be welcome at this kind of party. It might be better just to enjoy the event and make an appointment to chat about work with your boss at another time.

Office Party Type Three is perhaps the most 'dangerous' one, the traditional office knees-up. The trouble is that the line between business event and informal party isn't clear. The boss and directors seem to be off-duty and joining in the general fun. There is often free booze and people get carried away. We all know the awful things that happen at some office parties: getting drunk and trying to photocopy your bottom, snogging someone in the cupboard, not to mention becoming 'unwell' after a few too many beers. Watch out – some people you work with may be not so much your friends as your competitors and any gossip they spread will last a while. And, of course, the boss may have a rather long memory about what happened, too. Perhaps this is a bit cynical, but it always pays to behave in a civilised and in-control manner – you can still have fun and a drink or two, just watch it!

Formal occasions

There are many gatherings that are truly formal and serve a serious purpose. These may be business, academic, political or diplomatic functions and they are all subject to quite rigid 'rules of etiquette'. If you are going to dine in an Oxbridge college, a regimental mess, or as a guest of the Worshipful Company of Wig Makers (okay, that one's made up!) you really need to do your homework in advance. These places absolutely reek of tradition and there will be a hundred things you need to know. If what people think at such events matters to you, follow the accepted rules of their traditions. You can do so, even if you only follow them to help you feel more at ease. Happily, nowadays most of these bodies are well aware that their traditions appear somewhat arcane – not to mention stupid – to outsiders, so are helpful in explaining what's expected and not offended if you don't play the game.

What to wear

What do you wear if you're suddenly invited to some social occasion that is completely new to you? Does it matter? Well, ultimately no – it's you that's been invited, not your frock. But, naturally, it helps to feel that you're dressed for the occasion and not going to stand out like a sore thumb. There's nothing worse than turning up for a social occasion or a business meeting wearing very different clothes from the rest of the crowd – unless you like to create a stir of course! If you've seen the film *Bridget Jones' Diary*, you'll probably remember the scene where she turned up to what she thought was a tarts-and-vicars fancy dress do, only to find it was a formal reception.

Novelist Anthony Trollope once observed, 'I hold that gentleman to be the best dressed whose dress no one observes,' meaning that, in his opinion, the person who blends in with the crowd is the one who's dressed well for the occasion. Think about it: wearing clothes that fit the occasion will put you at your ease, but is also a courtesy to the host, who is no doubt anxious that things should go well, and that the whole event should be a success. That being said, only the most pompous host would complain if someone wearing jeans turned up at a formal wedding reception – it's the occasion that matters more than the clothing.

It seems to be a feature of film-star chic these days to blend casual and smart – jeans and diamonds, evening dresses and denim jackets. Not many people can get away with it and it's probably not a good idea to try for this look unless you're very sure you can carry it off. Play safe unless you have a model figure, and a budget to match.

Here are a few hints on what, in general, is considered acceptable dress for various situations. But you'll find plenty of situations where these 'rules' no longer apply, since life is much less rigid than it used to be only fifty years ago. But if you are worried about inadvertently causing offence, especially to people of an older generation, it might be worth considering these:

Gear for the men...

The suit – sometimes called a business suit, or a lounge suit – is the default 'smart' men's outfit. It's really a kind of unspoken 'uniform' for doing serious business and most suits are either dark grey or blue, sometimes with a pinstripe or chalk stripe to liven them up a bit. Green or brown suits are not generally very fashionable for conventional business wear. A suit can be a very expensive item, but need not be. If you're starting work in a big company, like a bank or law firm, you'll almost certainly be expected to wear a suit, even in this day and age. You'll probably have been told that normal work attire is 'suit and tie'.

The tie is not optional in a formal setting where 'suit and tie' is required. What the point of a tie is, nobody knows. It seems designed to be difficult to put on properly and then spend its time getting in the way. At least ties are a bit more adventurous today than they were a couple of generations ago when sober patterns and stripes were about all there was to choose from. Now you can get ties with silly cartoons, funky patterns and very 'loud' colours. But be careful – if your workplace is a serious one, a tie bearing a picture of Marilyn Monroe will probably not go down too well. Some people wear a tie indicating which school or Oxbridge university college they attended, but that is really rather a snobby and old-fashioned habit. But that's where the expression 'old school tie' comes from, a bit like referring to the 'old boys' network'.

Bow ties are a bit of a pain to get right. About the only time you'd be required to wear one is a formal wedding and then only if you are the groom, best man or one of the official ushers. The easiest way to tie a bow tie is to get somebody else to do it for you, or to get one that is ready tied, and attached to elastic!

Socks seem to be rather inoffensive wear, don't they? Well, clean ones, that is! But be careful in your choice – at a formal work place it may not be considered appropriate to wear brightly coloured socks, or socks with logos or pictures on them. Don't wear anything too flamboyant unless you are sure that it's acceptable.

For formal business wear, shirts should be white or blue, or a muted shade of pink also works. In general plain shirts are best for very conventional offices, but in others it may be quite okay to wear patterns and even very bright colours.

As a general rule of office-dress 'good manners', spend a few weeks getting the feel of how the office 'dress code' operates before you get out your silly socks and that tie with the flashing light on the end. (And in any case, you'd probably best save them for the office Christmas party.)

Evening wear

If you get an invitation to a formal dinner, it will usually say if 'evening dress' or 'black tie' is required. That's all very well, but what does it mean exactly? Both these mean that men should wear a dinner jacket (sometimes known as a tuxedo) and a black bow tie. Though actually, today, it is by no means essential to wear a black bow tie. Many people jazz up this rather sombre ensemble by wearing a colourful or patterned bow tie. In a tropical clime you might wear a white jacket instead of the more usual black, but this isn't usual otherwise.

So, that sorts out the gents, but what about the ladies? Formal evening dress for women is usually, but not always, long. You don't have to wear a fancy ball gown, but should make the effort to wear something quite smart. A formal knee-length dress is usually acceptable, if it is definitely the sort of thing you could class as 'evening wear' (usually made from something silky or velvety).

What other kinds of dress are there? Very rarely, today, you might be asked to a 'white tie' event. This means wearing tails – black, not white – and a white bow tie, for the men. Usually there's a special kind of white starched shirt, with a winged collar and a waistcoat. Many formal weddings adopt this dress – partly for the fun of it, more than convention! – and it is easiest to hire the lot for the evening. If you go to any gentlemen's outfitters or wedding-clothing hire place, they'll give you a great deal of helpful advice on what exactly to wear. For a 'white tie' event such as a state ball or similarly grand occasion, women would always wear long evening dresses, and often wear long white gloves as well.

For a 'white tie' event such as a state ball or similarly grand occasion, women would always wear long evening dresses, and often wear long white gloves as well.

Other types of dress sometimes specified are 'lounge suits', 'smart casual', 'informal' and 'business attire'. These are really to inform you that it isn't a very smart 'black tie' event, but you should just wear a suit (for 'lounge suit' or 'business attire') or a sports jacket and trousers, or something similar, if the event is casual. Jeans are probably not a good idea: a little bit *too* casual! For women, a suit or smart daywear for a 'business suit' event, and something smart, but more relaxed in other cases. In a way these invitations are most daunting, because there's no formal uniform

– just keep it smart but not too grand. If you wear a suit for a 'casual' occasions, that's not going to matter at all.

It certainly isn't deemed rude not to wear a hat, and very few occasions 'require' one – apart from a hard hat on a building site, of course!

An invitation may also indicate that 'decorations' may be worn. This, of course, refers to medals and other hardware you may have – military or civil awards etc. If you have any decorations of this kind, wear them on the left breast of your dinner jacket, when the occasion demands. If you are a woman, the left side of your evening dress or, if you are wearing a jacket, on the left breast. Incidentally, at some grand occasions women may be offered a corsage – this is simply a small spray of flowers.

Well, we hope that clears up what to wear! But, what if there is no indication of what to wear on your invitation? If you are any doubt, the best thing to do is to phone the host, or somebody else who is attending, and ask them. Then you can turn up confident that you're in the 'right' outfit for the occasion, and concentrate on enjoying it to the full.

Hats off – and on!

Not that long ago, all men wore hats, and you could actually tell quite a lot about a man by the hat he wore. Posh businessmen wore bowlers, less 'exalted' folks wore trilbies, and ordinary working-class people in more menial roles tended to wear flat caps. Of course, that's not the case at all today – you don't see many businessmen in bowlers and flat caps are all the fashion in some circles. It certainly isn't deemed rude not to wear a hat, and very few occasions 'require' one – apart from a hard hat on a building site, of course!

But there are a few simple rules of politeness if you do decide to wear a hat. If you're wearing a hat and go inside, you should take it off, especially if you are entering a house of worship (except in a synagogue or mosque, where the opposite applies, and you should keep your head covered). On very formal occasions, like smart society weddings and the Ascot races, top hats are still worn, by custom. You'll also need to wear a 'topper' if you're collecting an honour of some kind from the Queen. But apart from that, how you wear your hat, and if you choose to, is up to you – just take it off if you're in front of someone at the cinema, or you'll make no friends! It's no longer the case, as it was once, that men raise their hat with their left hand on meeting a lady (simultaneously extending their right hand to shake, quite a feat of co-ordination).

A word about healthy hat wearing. Sunhats in the burning sun, and woolly hats in the freezing winter winds are definitely a good idea. Other hats – especially the more 'amusing' or informal ones sported by the younger clientele, clubbers and snowboarders alike, may be best left to the young – but that's entirely up to you, you're as young as you feel, after all! In general, though, a multi-coloured velour clown hat with integral strobe lighting is probably inadvisable for picking up your OBE from the Queen.

Flat caps, panamas, bush hats and the rest are all perfectly acceptable in informal settings. The panama even makes it to the more formal settings of bowls, cricket and croquet. However, on the whole men are not expected to wear hats except on very formal occasions. So, if you're at all worried, it's probably best to leave your hat at home.

For the women, ladies' hat-wearing manners are a bit more of a challenge. Anything involving a religious ceremony may require a head covering of some kind for all the women, so a hat is advisable.

Certainly, today, you would not necessarily have to wear a hat at a Christian or civil ceremony wedding, for instance, but it depends on the formality involved. You would be expected to wear a hat at a formal event like racing at Ascot, or rowing at Henley, although the good news is that there's no strict 'rule' on what style it should be. Some women really go to town at this kind of event, and wear very grandiose confections, but you really don't need to. Most large department stores carry a wide range of hats suitable for more formal occasions, so just go along and try them all on for size.

The bling thing

Jewellery, and how and what to wear, is a difficult one – for those of us with strings of diamonds and reams of pearls to choose from! On the whole, what jewellery you wear for an occasion is simply a matter of your personal taste. 'Less is more' is usually a good rule, as a touch of understated but smart adornment can make its point, and look elegant and smart. There is no need to wear jewellery at all, unless you want to, but most women would probably wear a necklace and earrings for an evening 'do'.

Many men wear a wedding ring, and perhaps a signet ring too. Others wear a chain or medallion or perhaps a gold bracelet. None of this is 'required' or considered 'polite' (or not). Perhaps men loaded down with gold chains and medallions are more likely to be regarded as a bit of a 'medallion man' (not a compliment, generally) but, again, it's a matter of personal taste.

Rites of passage

Some call them 'hatches, matches and dispatches' – our social rites of passage are those formal occasions (such as christenings, engagements, weddings, funerals) that mark stages in our progress through life towards the inevitable. These important events are always formal in some sense, and have their own little rules of behaviour, which often come from long tradition. And we often like to preserve them, because it helps the event to feel special, after all.

Rites of passage can involve some sort of religious service or other expression of spiritual belief. In today's multi-cultural society that can be a bit intimidating for some of us, especially if we are unfamiliar with the faith involved. Quite often, only family and close friends are actually invited to the religious part of a ceremony and then a wider group of friends is invited to the evening party, or reception, that follows. That's one good way of helping everyone to feel at ease, and has the benefit of allowing people who feel uncomfortable with religion to miss that bit out.

If you get invited to a ceremony that is quite outside your own culture, you need to do a little research so that you'll know what to expect and how you should behave. For instance, at a Hindu ceremony men and women will not sit together. At a Jewish ceremony women should wear a hat or other head covering. If you're unsure what to expect, just ask the person who invited you: you'll find that most people love to tell you all about their customs and you may well end up with too much information, if anything! Usually you won't have to do anything too complicated other than observe the ceremony – remember, you were asked because your presence was valued. If the ceremony is being conducted in a foreign language, then you can either sit through it patiently, or get someone to translate.

Birth

The celebration of a baby's birth is generally an occasion of great joy. It gives not only the new parents, but all their friends and relatives, a chance to express their pleasure, show their support and wish the new offspring well as they embark on life. But even before birth, there's cause for celebration when a couple knows that they are 'expecting'. For reasons of both tradition and caution, however, it is usual not to throw a big 'baby shower' party to tell all your friends and relatives that you're going to have a baby until the first few months of pregnancy are past. Unfortunately, not all pregnancies make it past the three-month stage so, rather than get everyone excited and then have to give them bad news, it is usual to wait until the pregnancy is really going well. But of course, simply sharing the joy of your pregnancy with close friends and relatives is a different thing altogether.

Baby's here

All cultures are different and all individuals too. In some cultures women go into seclusion to give birth, while in others – like ours – the dad is fully able to take part in the delivery, and expected to as well. Some people even video the baby's birth. Who is present at the baby's birth, in addition to the medical staff, is more or less up to the parents.

Once the baby has been born, the new parents are likely to be inundated with friends and relations who wish to meet the new arrival. It can be a difficult time when sensitivity – basically good manners – towards the couple and their child can really help. If you're a friend, don't go rushing round immediately – your friend may need to spend quite a few days getting used to the experience. It's good manners just to send a card or a bouquet and get in touch a little later. And it's not just friends that need to be thoughtful – imagine that you're the new grandma and your daughter has just had her very first baby. You're overjoyed! And you have loads of experience of bringing up baby, so you just know that you'll be able to offer so much help and support. You'll be able to provide an expert hand in the baby's early days. But be careful: don't go taking over the situation. Your daughter (or son) now has a new family and needs to get used to the experience. Of course they are likely to appreciate and need your help – but they also need time for themselves and to learn how to look after their baby. And they may have some different ideas from you – remember to respect their wishes and bite your tongue if you would personally do things in another way. So take a back seat, be there when and if needed and express your love through respect and caring as much as child-care help.

New parents need to think about the feelings of the grandparents as well, of course. Think about it – it must make you feel rather strange to find your little girl or boy is really 'all grown up' and now has a baby of their own. They may suddenly feel very old indeed! Most people just love becoming grandparents – all the fun of young babies, without all the sleepless nights and nappy changing – but it can also be a rite of passage for them as well. They may even feel a bit 'useless' all of a sudden. Giving grandparents a role in the christening or naming ceremony can help make them feel better about any inner turmoil that may be going on.

Finally, perhaps you have a friend who's about to have a baby. Even if you personally aren't so keen on all that baby stuff – not everyone is – it's only good manners to show some interest in your friend's big event. Try asking when the baby's due, whether the parents know if it's a girl or boy (and, if so, whether they are telling), and if they have names they're thinking of. Your friend will appreciate your good manners in showing an interest, and giving them a chance to chat about what, for them, is a hugely significant event. And after the baby's born, it's normal to send greetings cards, flowers and cuddly toys for the baby, if you know either or both of the parents quite well.

Making the announcement

If you're the one who's expecting, feel free just to give out as much information as you're comfortable with. You don't have to involve everyone in your choice of names, unless you want to, or tell them if it's going to be a boy or girl. But it's good manners to make an announcement of the birth – usually in your local paper, where there's a special section that doesn't cost much and is sometimes even free. And of course, do phone family and close friends to let them know about your happy event. It's also quite acceptable to send a 'round robin' email to work colleagues, or a wider circle of friends – or even, if you're that way inclined, put together a little web page with pictures of you and your new baby (but probably not clips from the video of the birth!).

Christenings and baby-namings

It wasn't that long ago that a christening was a ceremony almost every new-born British baby experienced – some of them crying throughout as the 'holy water' was administered. Today christenings are far less common and it's no longer a sign of social stigma not to be christened. Indeed, many people who are not practising Christians think it rather hypocritical to have their baby christened in a church. Other people like to have the ceremony, despite not being Christians, and many churches are sympathetic. Many other people, of course, have their baby named in a ceremony appropriate to their own, different religion, while people with no religious views can choose to have a non-religious, secular baby-naming ceremony, like that of the Humanist Society.

Whatever the ceremony is like, there will be certain expectations of how people behave and it's likely to require informal but smart attire – perhaps a suit and tie, or something similarly dressed up, for the chaps, and maybe a smart dress or trouser suit, even a hat, for women. Life, and the ceremonies that go with it, is so varied nowadays that it's best to go for smart but not too formal, unless the invitation says otherwise.

Perhaps you have been asked to be a godparent? In the Christian religion, the godparents are expected to be confirmed in the Christian faith, and their role is to guide and support the child's religious upbringing. Godparents are usually longstanding friends of the child's parents and, in practice, don't get 'tested at the door' to see if they are Christian through and through. It's more important to be someone who'll offer support, love and friendship. So, if you are not a Christian but are asked to be a godparent, don't feel you have to say no.

Most people regard the request to be a godparent as a great honour and are delighted to accept. If, however, you don't feel willing or able to be a godparent, you need to be very careful how you decline the invitation. As it's such an important request from the parents, it needs a serious-minded excuse. It's good manners to explain that you maybe don't feel you can, on religious or personal grounds, although you are extremely honoured to have been asked. Whatever your reason, make sure that you speak in person with the parents, and thank them for thinking of you.

A christening is a good excuse for a party and it is usual for the guests to bring the baby a present. Christening presents are usually rather formal and are often things that the child will need in later life. Bibles and prayer books used to be popular, as did silver christening spoons (thus giving rise to the expression 'to be born with a silver spoon in your mouth'). But really, any thoughtful and appropriate gift will be fitting – usually, people buy something that lasts. If you go into any large department store you'll find a gift section expressly for christening and baby-naming events – just ask a member of staff to guide you through what's available.

First communions, confirmations and bar mitzvahs

These religious ceremonies – the first two Christian, the last Jewish – are examples of ceremonies that mark a stage at which a child is considered, in some sense, to have become grown up. First communion is a Roman Catholic ceremony and usually takes place at the age of eight. Confirmation is particularly popular in Protestant churches and may take place at any age, though it is most popular for children in their early teens. A bar mitzvah is a ceremony by which a Jewish boy of thirteen is formally accepted as an adult member of the community. There is a version of the ceremony for girls known as a bat mitzvah but it is far less common.

As a guest at one of these ceremonies, or any other informal version of the same kind of event, you'll need to bring an appropriate gift. How much you spend is entirely up to you, and if you are not a very close friend of the family, you shouldn't feel you have to purchase an extremely generous present. But a box of chocolates won't cut it here! Some events may even have a 'gift list', or you can give some money in the form of a gift certificate, or book token perhaps. If in doubt, ask somebody else you know who is going what sort of thing they recommend, or ask in a shop that sells gifts.

What do you wear? Well, usually these kinds of occasions are pretty formal. Suits for men, smart trousers or dresses for women, possibly hats as well. Remember, if you aren't Jewish but are invited to the synagogue bit of a bar mitzvah you will need something to cover your head. For women, buying a hat is perhaps still more usual, while men may not know what kind of hat is suitable – a baseball cap isn't going to work here! You will need to find something sufficiently dignified. At a Jewish ceremony you can wear a *yarmulke* (the skull cap worn by Jewish men), even if you're not Jewish yourself – that's fine, and will be seen as a sign of respect, not an insult. You may even be offered one if you arrive without headgear. No one will mind that you are wearing one if you are not Jewish; in fact people will be happy that you made an effort to join in. You can even put a (clean!) hankie over your hair if that's all you have – as an accepted emergency measure!

Fortunately, guests at these kinds of 'growing-up' ceremonies don't have much to do except stand around watching the proceedings, and enjoying the party. However, there are things you should know beforehand, so that you show good manners. For instance – what is the attitude to photography or video recording? In many places of worship this is not acceptable inside, and certainly you should always ask beforehand in any case. Also, make sure you don't get in the way of any professional photographer who may have been hired to record the occasion. At all formal family occasions, it's best to check with the hosts – in advance, not at the time – if they mind, especially during a ceremony. This applies as much to weddings.

Engagements and weddings

It's a long while since the time when being an unmarried couple 'living out of wedlock' was considered quite unacceptable in British society. Today you can marry, in a civil or religious ceremony of your choice, or you can live together as common law man and wife, or as a gay couple, male or female. That's up to you, and you don't need to feel that society is pushing you into an arrangement that doesn't suit you, or fit your beliefs. However, the Christian tradition of marriage persists as both a genuine religious ceremony, for many, or more of a superficial celebration for others. And both religious and civil marriages are often followed by formal wedding receptions, which have quite traditional social rules and formats.

The Christian tradition of marriage persists as both a genuine religious ceremony, for many, or more of a superficial celebration for others.

It used to be that the young man asked his sweetheart's father for his daughter's 'hand in marriage'. If you find anyone who's actually done this recently, do let us know! Most prospective father-in-laws today are hardly expecting to make decisions on their daughter's behalf (and most daughters probably wouldn't let them!).

Another rather old-fashioned formality is that of going down on one knee to ask the girl to marry you. That one does still happen, as a romantic gesture that's maybe a little self-conscious. It's certainly not compulsory.

'Popping the question' used to be the man's job, and it's still, traditionally, that way. Women only got a chance to do it during a Leap Year, traditionally. Things are changing and women are just as able to ask a man to marry them. Every couple is different, and who asks who is less important than deciding that you want to formalise your loving relationship and celebrate this choice with friends and family.

The 'manners' required for asking someone to marry you are simple – ask, lovingly and sincerely, in whatever way is natural to your relationship. Perhaps the only difficulty is how to say 'no' to a proposal. Saying 'no' doesn't mean that you don't care for a person, or don't respect them – spend time explaining, gently and carefully, just why marrying is not for you. Remember, asking someone to marry you is a huge moment, that takes a bit of nerve – if you're the one who's saying 'no', say so with consideration.

Once the question has been popped and accepted, there is still usually a period of engagement before the wedding happens. And engagement conventionally involves the giving of rings. Traditionally the man gave the woman a ring when he made his proposal, but it's more normal to choose an engagement ring together, or even to buy and exchange rings so that you can both wear one. You can, if you want, announce your engagement by a notice placed in a newspaper. However, informing people of an engagement is a fairly relaxed business and many people are content to let the word get around on the

Informing people of an engagement is a fairly relaxed business and many people are content to let the word get around on the grapevine.

grapevine. Some people hold an engagement party to announce the happy news to all their friends and relatives. This can be a jolly, relaxed occasion at which people do pretty much as they wish. It isn't nearly as formal as the average wedding party.

What if things go wrong, and you and your partner decide to break off the engagement? It's actually not that unusual for a relationship to get a bit shaky once the engagement has been announced and the pressure to organise a wedding is on. It can feel very awkward if your parents and friends are all rooting for you, and you don't want to disappoint them. They may even have spent money on your behalf, booking the reception or arranging the food. But think about it – this is one case where your future happiness is more important than the inconvenience you may cause. Talk to your family and explain that the marriage is going to make you unhappy. But if the engagement is called off, you should let people know. If they have already sent you presents, you need to send these back, with a brief letter of apology. You don't have to go into great detail about what went wrong, simply say that you are sorry for any inconvenience and hope they'll understand. And true friends will, of course.

In general, once you're engaged, wedding preparations begin. A wedding, or other similar celebration, is probably one of the most emotionally charged occasions most of us will go through. It involves not only the happy couple but their immediate families, relations and friends. It is an occasion when emotions are not only heightened but also very mixed. The formality of the conventional wedding and wedding reception can actually help this very powerful event to go well.

Wedding preparations

Let's assume for the moment that the wedding will be held either in church or a registry office. There are plenty of other possibilities, among them mosques, synagogues, temples and civil ceremonies in exotic venues at home and abroad. If you get invited to a ceremony that is in a faith you don't have experience of, try to make discreet enquiries of your host, well in advance, about the nature of the ceremony.

For a conventional Christian-tradition wedding, one of the first jobs for the bride and groom is to choose the bridesmaids and best man. It is important to find your bridesmaids early on because you will need to buy or make dresses for all of them and this can take time. Bridesmaids are traditionally any age from small children up to young women; if married they are called a 'matron of honour'. Wearing a pretty dress is more or less what the whole ceremony is about as far as a bridesmaid is concerned. She doesn't have to do much except follow the bride into the church (carrying her train if she has one). As she is likely to be a relative or close friend of the bride, she will also be valued for the moral support she provides on such a big day.

The prospective husband, or groom, has the 'best man' to give him support. Unlike the bridesmaids, the best man has quite a few duties to perform, in the traditional role. The groom can choose anyone to take this role, usually a very close friend or a brother. It can be quite a difficult choice, for which diplomacy is needed. Since your best man is going to have to make a speech, look after some of the organising and also produce the ring during the service, you don't want somebody who – however good a friend – might be a bit unreliable. If you're choosing a best man, bear in mind the other male friends and relatives who may, even at the back of their mind, be hoping you'll choose them – and find a way of easing the situation. 'You know, I chose Bob because he's also a friend of Carrie's,' or 'Jack's one of my oldest friends from school, and I promised him years ago I'd do the same for him.'

Who pays for the wedding? That's something that is likely to be on your mind, if you're about to get spliced! Traditionally, the bride's parents used to pay for the whole wedding and reception. Often, today, both the bride's and the groom's parents split the cost, or the bride and groom pay for it themselves – especially if they are older and both working. If you're going to get married and pay for it yourself, do bear in mind that actually your parents might like to feel involved and contribute financially – offer them the chance to pay for something like the dress, or the honeymoon, or whatever you feel would be within their means.

Who wears what? The traditional 'white wedding' used to be only for virgin brides, but that's certainly no longer strictly enforced. Some second marriages, and some very obviously pregnant brides, are still white. It really doesn't matter, although at a very traditional church you might find the vicar has strong views. Some brides, especially at winter weddings, go the other way and choose rich colours like dark red, or blue.

The groom and male guests at a traditional wedding tend to wear suits. At a formal wedding (or even an informal one, where you want the fun of it), top hats and tails might even be worn by the groom and his best man – what's sometimes known as 'morning dress'. In this case the father of the bride, and the male ushers, would wear morning dress as well. You don't have to buy it of course; that sort of outfit can be hired for the day.

Normally, if you have chosen a traditional Christian church wedding, you would meet with the vicar in advance. This is only good manners, as a courtesy, but is also so that the vicar may talk with you about your spiritual and religious beliefs. Some vicars may give you advice on marriage and what it entails, after the big day. Most vicars will understand that you may not be a regular church-goer, but have beliefs that concur with the Christian religion, and would like to mark your commitment in church. When you meet the vicar you will also choose the music and hymns to sing at the ceremony. You'll also need to meet to have a 'rehearsal' at the church, about a week before the wedding, usually with all the 'principal players' – the parents of bride and groom, bridesmaids etc – but not 'in costume'. It's good manners to turn up, on time, and to take it seriously – because it's designed to help your big day go smoothly.

Wedding ceremonies

Wedding 'manners' are quite carefully defined by tradition. It won't be the end of the world if things don't go quite to plan, but here is the traditional order of progress for a Christian church wedding and it's often the same for a more formal civil wedding.

The bridegroom and his best man should be first to arrive at the wedding venue and take up their places at the front of the church or room. Ushers, chosen from close friends and relatives, help guide arriving guests to their places. Traditionally, they will ask guests whether they are there for the bride or the groom. Today, many people are likely to be there for both – so feel free to say that, if asked. In a formal wedding, the bride's friends are seated behind her (usually on the left side of the church) and the groom's behind him (on the right side of the venue). But it's far more usual today for people to sit wherever they wish, especially in civil ceremonies. If you have small children that might make a noise, it's good manners to ask if you can sit near the back, or on an outside aisle, perhaps – so that you can make a quick escape if little Johnny begins to wail just as the vows are being made.

The bride traditionally arrives a little late, just to make sure everyone is ready, really. At a traditional church wedding, she comes 'down the aisle' on her father's arm and he leads her to stand before the altar then takes a step back. The best man should normally have charge of the rings and make sure that he is ready to hand them to the groom when he needs them. When the vicar or celebrant asks who is giving the woman in marriage, the bride's father indicates that he is the one.

If you're the one getting married, do make sure your answers can be heard. It's not a private moment as much as a public declaration that you are sharing with your friends and families. It's quite in order to look happy, and smile – but it isn't good manners to interrupt the vicar or celebrant (or to break into nervous giggles). Services today are very flexible and often the bride and groom write their own vows and read them to each other – these can be personal, and informal, and need not be religious. So if you have spent a long while thinking of what to say, make sure everyone can hear it.

> *If you're the one getting married, do make sure your answers can be heard. It's not a private moment as much as a public declaration.*

At a church wedding, the ceremony ends when you sign the register. There's a similar moment in a civil wedding. After that, you're married and can either walk down the aisle happily, or go to mingle with your guests, or whatever is appropriate. Remember, if you have hired a photographer, it's good manners to let them do their job properly. This will probably be the time when they want you to pose for photographs in various groups. However excited you are, take the time to do this well – the photographs will be with you for a long time!

A well-known wedding tradition is for the bride to turn her back and throw her wedding bouquet over her shoulder, towards the bridesmaids (usually). The old wives' tale attached used to be that the person who caught it would be next to get married. It isn't compulsory today and may happen instead at the reception. If you're the bride, throw it towards someone who'll appreciate this special memento – perhaps the chief bridesmaid, or even your mum. If you're a guest, don't make a rugby tackle for it!

Receptions and speeches

The reception is the place where things can, and often do, go wrong, so it is important to know the rules and make sure that the other participants know them as well. First, it's only polite that the happy couple should get to the venue before the guests so that they are there to welcome them on arrival. Many people have a formal receiving line in which the bride, groom and immediate family members line up to shake hands with each guest as they arrive, but don't feel obliged. If you want to be really grand you can have someone call out their names as they approach the line. This may seem rather too formal, but it does ensure that each guest is welcomed personally. If you are the bride or groom, or one of the parents, just behave as any good party host would – circulate, make sure people are happy and looked after. Don't forget, wedding parties are unusual because there will be many people there who don't know anyone else. It's a little daunting to socialise for such a long period with complete strangers, so take time to work out a good seating plan or to introduce people to each other. At a buffet-type meal the family members should circulate to ensure that all the guests are being looked after. And do keep an eye on Uncle Stan, who gets a bit boring once he's had a drink or two – rescue his latest 'captive audience' from him occasionally!

Presenting the presents

At a formal wedding, the guests will, normally, bring or send a present. You won't be expected to open them then and there. Instead, write every single person a thank-you letter, very soon after you return from your honeymoon (if you have one). In this case good manners dictate that you should send a handwritten note, on attractive paper or a note card. Make sure to say you much you liked the gift (whatever you thought of it!) and provide a few words about your honeymoon, or the event itself. Say how nice it was to see the person, if they came to the wedding.

As a guest, it is good manners to provide a nice gift, wrapped and with a congratulatory card. Something useful for the home is always a good bet, and need not be too expensive – perhaps a set of wine glasses, or a tablecloth. You can send this in advance, normally to the home of the person who invited you (the parents of the bride, traditionally) or bring it to the reception, where there will probably be a table to leave gifts on. Do make sure to say who the gift is from!

Once people have eaten and drunk enough, the speeches begin. At a traditional wedding they go in this order:

- Father of the bride (who also toasts the happy couple).
- The groom thanks his father-in-law (and others) and proposes a toast to the bridesmaids.
- The best man replies on behalf of the bridesmaids and also reads out any messages from those who could not be present.

Although this is the traditional order, it is quite permissible to vary it – today, many brides would like to make a speech as well, and there's no reason why they shouldn't!

If you're one of the people required to give a speech, don't panic – there are quite a few books on wedding etiquette and speeches, so pop down to the library.

Basically, the bridegroom's speech is a simple thank-you to everyone for everything. Don't miss anyone out – you'll hurt their feelings. Remember to sneak in a 'my wife and I' at some point – you're bound to get a cheer!

The best man has a more difficult job, since he needs to say something gently amusing about his old friend, the bridegroom – perhaps a story about a childhood jape, or some other anecdote. Above all, don't really embarrass the groom – or the bride – and don't reveal any really personal secrets.

And now for the fun – if there's to be dancing, the bride and groom should start things with a dance together, after which everyone joins in. Formal dances are rare nowadays, so really there are no rules on what is good manners (stay upright, don't drink too much!). But it is traditional for the bride to dance with her dad at some point.

Near the end of the reception the bride will disappear to go and get changed, and then the happy couple will leave, usually to go off on honeymoon. The best man and other friends of the groom usually take this opportunity to decorate their car with shaving foam and streamers. Once the bride and groom have left, the party often continues for a while and people then start going home. But, again, today there are no strict rules – many couples don't see why they should leave early to 'go away', and enjoy staying on to the end of the evening with everyone else.

As bride and groom, it's essentially good manners to buy a little thank-you present for the bridesmaids and the best man, something bigger than a box of chocolates – perhaps a bottle of good wine or Scotch, or silk scarves or jewellery for the bridesmaids. And perhaps something more modest for all the people who helped out as ushers, or volunteered to help with food.

Today, church wedding receptions and civil ceremony receptions are often identical, it's only the ceremony itself that differs slightly, although there can certainly be singing and music at both. For a church wedding, it's good manners to invite the vicar to the reception. You can also invite the registrar, in a civil ceremony, but there is less obligation to do so.

Although we've concentrated on how a traditional church or civil wedding and party proceeds, there are of course many other different kinds of religious ceremonies. All weddings are similar in that the two people getting married are the centre of attention and are there to publicly make vows as to their commitment to each other. Whoever the people are, and whatever the religion, enjoy the ceremony as a time of joy shared with friends and family. And, even if you don't know what is going on – or don't personally agree with it – it's good manners to follow the accepted protocol and kneel or stand when everyone else does, join in the hymns (if you can) and generally take the whole thing as seriously as it is intended.

Lastly, don't forget that however happy the occasion, it is a time of great emotion. Many new 'mum-in-laws' are actually feeling mixed joy and sadness, at losing their son or daughter to a 'new life'. So respect that people may be feeling rather tense or emotional and use your good manners to be calm and respectful to all, without taking offence at any unintended words.

Significant others

Modern manners entail understanding modern lifestyles. Don't forget that, however traditional your own family might be, others may come from very different situations. Many people divorce and remarry today, and there is no stigma attached to that at all. People of the same gender set up home together, some people choose not to have a family, some have large 'blended' families from different marriages. Good manners today means being sensitive to the fact that not everyone will have the same family situation as you are familiar with, and that doesn't make their lifestyle better or worse than yours. In general, if you are not sure how to refer to someone, ask tactfully – if you are close enough to one of the family. But it's easiest to avoid blunders simply by referring to 'partners' or 'significant others'.

Don't forget that, however traditional your own family might be, others may come from very different situations.

One of the problems is that, as we have observed elsewhere, we now tend to deal with almost everyone on a first-name basis and it means that we have no clue as to the precise way in which people are related. To make things even more complicated, there may be children, step-children, half-brothers and half-sisters all living under the same roof. The trouble is that if you ask all the questions to which you may urgently need answers, then you risk looking nosey. If you don't ask, you risk making assumptions that prove not only incorrect but embarrassingly wrong. There are no rules about this, but I can give you, from personal experience, a very good tip: ask your kids. They usually have far fewer hang-ups about it all, and know just who's living with who, and whose kids are whose.

If you are in an unconventional relationship – or one that might seem unconventional to someone of an older generation – it's good manners to make sure that they have some help. 'Jane's my partner' or 'well, we don't use "step-children", they're all just "the kids" to us'. If you are recently divorced, it's particularly important to ensure that people you may not have seen for some time are aware of this, to help them avoid a blunder. And if they do assume you're still married, don't take offence – they just didn't know. And never ask your friends to choose between you and your 'ex'. Why on earth should they?

Funerals

Unlikely though it may seem, there are good funerals and bad funerals. A good one demonstrates the love that those left behind feel for the deceased. It also gives everyone a chance to express their love and support for those who are bereaved. The ceremony needs to be dignified and well organised. This means that all the participants know what is expected of them. It may be a staple comedy situation on TV, but in real life there are few things more upsetting than a funeral that goes wrong.

There are practical and legal requirements that you will need to investigate separately, but here are some of the things that good manners require:

- First, if you are the next of kin you need to tell people the sad news as soon as possible. Relations and close friends of the deceased should be informed by phone or, if that is not possible, by a handwritten letter. Email should only be used in dire emergency.
- If the deceased was still working then, of course, the employer should be informed by phone at the earliest opportunity.
- Once those most closely concerned have been informed it is usual to place an announcement in the national and/or local press. This should not only give the information that a death has occurred but should also tell people where and

when the funeral will be held. If you want flowers to be sent you must state where they are to go. If you would prefer people to make a charitable contribution instead of flowers you should tell them which charity you are supporting. You might want to appoint someone to collect all the money and send it as one sum in memory of your loved one.

- You should also write to any social organisations (clubs, associations, charities, etc) with which the deceased was connected. This is not only polite but it will minimise the risk of you receiving upsetting mail and phone calls in the months to come.

- Some people hold a viewing at which people can go to see the deceased and pay their last respects. This used to be done in the deceased's home but that custom is now rare, except in certain communities. Usually the viewing is held at a chapel of rest.

- All practical aspects of the funeral will be organised by the undertaker, but he will need some help from the next of kin. For example, some people regard it as essential that the hearse should start its journey to the funeral from the deceased's home. They will also hire funeral cars and close relatives and friends will be invited to ride in the cortège. It is vital that people are told in advance whether they are expected to go in a funeral car and, if so, in which one. Traditionally the closer you were to the deceased, the nearer your car will be to the hearse. Nowadays, however, some people prefer not to have a cortège and for the hearse to arrive at the funeral straight from the undertaker's premises. There are no rules about which approach you take – it is entirely a matter of personal preference.

74

- Funerals can take many forms and it is essential that you let people know what sort yours is going to be. You don't need to do this formally, but you should let your friends and relatives spread the word. If you are attending a funeral and aren't sure what to wear, simply wear smart clothes in dark colours – black, nowadays, is not essential, although it's traditionally the colour of mourning. Full mourning dress – black tails and hat, formal dresses – is rarely worn, and the invitation would say if it was required. If the funeral is an especially tragic one (that of a child or young person, for example) it is unlikely that people will be feeling anything other than wretched. However, where the deceased has had a long, fulfilled and happy life there may well be an element of celebration involved. So it's as well for people to know how they are expected to act. I went to the funeral of a man who had led a full, active life, had been happily married twice and had loads of nice children and grandchildren. His passing was seen as the inevitable bittersweet end of his life and people celebrated it as such.

- The actual service can take just about any form you wish. You do not have to have a religious service. Instead, you could have close friends and relatives sharing their memories of the deceased and readings from favourite poems. The only thing you can't do is to have no ceremony at all. If you don't provide a ceremony the duty vicar will be called in to say a few words. There is absolutely no right or wrong way to organise a funeral. All the decisions are entirely personal and depend on the view of the next of kin.

- As a guest it is essential good manners to treat the whole occasion with seriousness and respect, whatever you may think of the ceremony, or the deceased. Even if you are nervous, refrain from whispering with your neighbours, or breaking into giggles if a particularly awful choice of music comes up.

- It is usual for the mourners to gather at the church or crematorium. The closest relatives and friends will go around welcoming people and thanking them for coming. Someone will remain with the deceased's partner to give moral support. When you are summoned for the funeral to begin you should walk quietly into the church and be seated. Sometimes, a man may offer a female guest his arm, to walk in with her. This should be taken for what it is – a traditional and slightly old-fashioned example of supportive good manners.

- The deceased's closest family and friends will occupy seats nearest the front and others will fit in behind as best they can. If you are not a close friend or family member, don't sit near the front.

- After the ceremony, it is usual to thank the vicar or whoever else performed the rites. Some people may have travelled a long way to the funeral and will be feeling wretched and quite probably cold. Therefore, guests (including the vicar) are normally invited to take refreshment somewhere. This can be at the deceased's home or it may be at a local hotel or in a room hired in a pub. At this point the conversation can become less gloomy. There is no hard-and-fast rule for how to behave on this occasion and you will have to take your lead from those around you.

If you were not close enough to the deceased to attend the funeral, but you are acquainted with the family, you should send a card of condolence or, better still, visit to give your condolences in person. A small gift, such as flowers or a plant, is customary.

You may be daunted about talking with someone who has suffered a recent bereavement, and even want to avoid them, but do take the trouble to give them your support and show your considerate good manners in just popping round to see how they are doing. Remember that they may well be feeling extremely lonely and wretched, and even a few minutes' conversation may be a great comfort to them. As always, good manners are a case of putting the other person first, even if you feel a little awkward.

Eating Out

Eating out – especially on unusually formal occasions – can be a surprisingly nerve-racking activity. That's a shame, because it should, after all, be a pleasure. So here are some clues on the 'rules' of good manners in some of the grander situations you might find yourself in.

Formal dining

Taking your place

At many formal parties, such as a wedding or a retirement meal, perhaps, there will probably be some milling around before people proceed to their seats. This period is sometimes called a 'reception' or simply 'drinks', and drinks are usually served – most likely by people coming around with trays, or perhaps glasses of wine will be laid out on a table for you to help yourself to one. Really, this time is a chance for the guests to mingle informally and get to know each other. It also gives you a chance to have a quick glass of something, if that helps you feel less nervous – but don't overdo it, the evening has only just begun! There may be a seating plan on display and, if so, you should take the opportunity to work out where you are sitting. At some point you will be invited to go into dinner and, if the affair is really old-fashioned, gentlemen will offer a lady their arm to hold while they lead them in. But more likely, everyone will meander in informally to take their seats.

If there is no seating plan then you may find that name cards have been put at each place setting. Try to find your card with minimum fuss. It is certainly not good manners to rearrange the place cards to sit next to someone you'd rather talk to. You should sit where you have been placed, and show your good manners by saying hello to the people on your table, making introductions if you don't know them – you don't have to wait to be introduced, just say 'Hello, I'm John Baker, I don't believe we've met,' and offer your hand to shake. A thoughtful host will have spent time on arranging the seating so that people with interests in common, or who might well like each other, are seated together.

When you've found your seat, it's quite all right to simply sit down when it seems everyone else around you is settling. It's no longer the case that men must wait until all women present are seated, or stand and pull back the woman's chair for her to sit on. You can certainly follow these old-school customs if you like, but they are a little outdated, and might even cause offence.

Don't talk with your mouth full

Formal dinners are as much about conversation as they are about food, so a general rule is to cut your food into small chunks that can be chewed easily and swallowed quickly when required. However good the food is, don't simply concentrate on eating and ignore your companions. Make sure that you are eating slowly and carefully enough to be able to make conversation with others on your table. It's good manners to include everyone near you in any conversation, and be especially careful to speak to anyone who looks a bit left out or shy, perhaps on their own. Ask them occasional questions: 'so, Elspeth, what do you do for a living?' or 'Jim, have you been working at Barnards' for long now?'. Similarly, try to steer the conversation to other topics if someone seems to have taken it over with talk about themselves. Treat the table as a mini-dinner party, where you are an attentive and interested guest.

Do make sure you have introduced yourself, or been introduced, to everyone seated with you. If you forget someone's name, as often happens when you meet several new people at once, you can say 'I'm sorry, your name just slipped my mind...it's...?' and the person will usually take the hint and tell you.

Saying grace

In some places, especially the colleges of the older universities, it is customary for grace to be said before the meal begins. Grace is a Christian (usually) custom in which God is 'thanked' for the food and company. This may be in Latin, if you're at one of the grander Oxbridge colleges. Whether you are a believer or not, you should bow your head slightly until it is over. Bear in mind when you first approach the table that you may need to remain standing and wait for grace to be said. Just watch what everyone else is doing.

Conversation

Formal dinners are far more than a chance to have some good food. They're an opportunity for people to relax and socialise in pleasant surroundings, in a kind of civilised bonding exercise. So keep conversation light and friendly: it's not the place for talking shop with colleagues.

At a large dinner, the host doesn't have a hope of keeping track of the conversation and steering it away from boring or even controversial topics. As a guest, your good manners can help you to assist here. Always talk to both the diners either side of you, not just the one who you get on best with. Don't sit in silence, however shy you are. Anyway, you'll enjoy the event more if you make an effort to take part, even if you dread small talk. Just smile a lot, ask general questions of your fellow diners, about their lives and interests, and be prepared to chat a little about yours. Don't feel that your life is uninteresting or boring, simply because it seems so different from the person's next to you. And show interest in what people tell you about themselves: you may be surprised what you learn about life!

Bread and rolls

In more formal dinners and restaurants bread is either brought to your table by the waiter, or is already on the table, usually in a basket in the middle. Or you may find a bread roll placed on your side plate (that's the small plate to your left). You can eat it as soon as the starter is served. It's good manners to offer the basket of bread around to your near neighbours before taking one yourself.

If you're being fussy about 'etiquette', it's normal to cut a slice of bread into pieces with a knife but for a roll (or bread if you wish), you should tear it into conveniently sized pieces, which you butter as you eat them. But that's just custom: whatever you choose is fine. Usually butter will be on a plate with a butter knife to take some with. Don't use this knife to cut your own bread – simply take the butter and put the knife back.

Don't throw your bread rolls at your neighbour, unless it's a very good party!

The staff

A big formal dinner do will probably have waiting staff. Their job is to be as near invisible as possible, and just make sure everything you need is there. It's a little different from a restaurant waiter, who may be keen to give you lots of information and advice on what to order or drink, and will hope for a nice tip too. You don't have to tip staff at a formal dinner, or even speak to them much as they serve you, although the occasional word of thanks as they deliver your next course or fill your glass is just fine, and good manners after all.

If something is wrong, don't make a big fuss. Simply speak quietly to the waiter nearest you. There's no need to be angry or speak loudly, just say 'I'm rather sorry, but this fish isn't quite done – do you think you could cook it a bit more?' or something similarly polite.

Special meals

Perhaps you are a vegetarian, or allergic to seafood or gluten, or have a religion that doesn't permit you to eat certain foods. If so, it's good manners to make sure your hosts know well in advance, so that suitable arrangements can be made. Don't leave it until you arrive, or even the day before – it will cause the host embarrassment if they can't produce a meal for you, and even a vegetarian meal is still an unusual option to some people, especially perhaps the older generation. So, think ahead and give the host a quick phone call or drop them a note to say 'I'm vegetarian, so thought I'd better let you know now' or 'By the way, just to let you know I only eat halal food, do let me know if I can suggest anything simple the caterer could provide'.

Incidentally, it is perfectly acceptable to refuse food on dietary or ethical grounds, but it is not okay to decline a whole course simply because you don't like the look of it. Even if you have an extreme dislike of apples, and an apple pie turns up for the dessert course, you'll have to make a stab at it, to be polite. Eat a few mouthfuls (a glass of water can help you get it down!) without showing any dislike, and perfect the art of 'picking' a bit at the rest, and moving it around the plate until the course is over and you can put it aside.

Navigating the place setting

Cutlery

A fully laden dining table groaning with cutlery, porcelain, silver and flowers is a magnificent, and, to some, intimidating, sight, but there is really no need to feel dazzled by all that silverware. Even if your normal meal of choice is a double cheeseburger with fries, you can still easily find your way around the formal dining table.

Like everything else, it's simple once you know how. Look at the cutlery and you'll see that everything will have been laid out for you in the right order – all you have to do is work your way inwards from the outer items. At the outside, there may be a small knife for you to butter your bread and then a small knife and fork to use on the starter. There may also be a soup spoon (more rounded than a normal spoon) in case you need it. Your main knife and fork will be closest to where your plate is set down, so if in doubt, look at those and work outwards. Cutlery for desserts might be at the top of your place setting or might be supplied by the staff when your dessert is brought. If you drop an item of cutlery, you can simply ask the waiting staff if they could please bring you another. In general, don't go grovelling under the table to pick it up unless it is very near (and the floor is very clean!)

The 'correct' way to hold a knife is in your right hand with the handle tucked into the palm of your hand; your thumb extends down one side of the handle and the forefinger points down the back (not touching the blade), with the remaining fingers curled around the handle. When a fork is used with a knife, it is held in the left hand with the tines – that's the prongs – pointing downward. Hold the handle near the tip rather than near the base. When using a fork by itself, it can be held the other way, with the tines pointing upward. The American custom of cutting up all one's food and then using the fork to shovel it up may be frowned upon by sticklers for dining etiquette in very grand establishments, but is usually acceptable otherwise – more and more of us eat that way nowadays. When using a spoon and fork to eat pudding, the fork should again be held tines down. Like forks, spoons are held near the tip of the handle. There, that's how to hold cutlery in very grand style!

Napkins

The napkin that's for your use will be on your left, probably on your side plate. Or it may be in the middle of your dinner plate, or in your water glass, folded into a fancy arrangement. As soon as you sit down, take it and spread it across your lap. Do not, in any circumstances, tuck it into the neck of your shirt, even if that seems much more sensible and you always do that at home! The exception is that if especially messy food (such as lobster) is to be served you may be provided with a suitable bib to protect your clothing, or alternatively everyone may tuck their napkin in. In this case only, if in doubt, look to see what everyone else is doing. But in more usual formal dinners you only use the napkin to clean your fingers and dab excess food from around your mouth. Don't make a big fuss of it. At the end of the meal it is usual to leave the napkin unfolded – just crumpled up and on, or near, your plate. It's one way of showing the waiting staff that you have finished.

Too many glasses!

At a very classy dinner there may be all kinds of glasses on the table by your plate. But there will also probably be all kinds of waiting staff, and they will fill your glass for you – so, don't worry, they will choose the right one for you. But sometimes at big meals the wine is left on each table for diners to serve themselves. Then, it can be helpful to know what kinds of drinks go in what kinds of glasses. Here are some pointers:

- Red wine glasses are usually larger and rounder than those used for white wine. You should not fill more than one third of the glass. The glass is only large so that the aroma, or 'bouquet', of the wine can be appreciated more fully.
- White wine is poured into rather slender glasses. Again, you should not over-fill your glass. White wine is usually served chilled and you will be supplied with a container of ice to keep the wine cold. Return the bottle to the ice after you have poured the wine.
- Champagne is served in tall, narrow glasses called 'flutes'.
- Port is drunk from small wine glasses and brandy glasses are very big and balloon-shaped. Again, you shouldn't fill a brandy glass up – a small amount in the bottom is sufficient.
- There will also be a water glass somewhere. It might look like a tumbler, but some places will just give you a spare wine glass.

It is polite to keep an eye on your fellow guests' glasses and offer to refill them from time to time, but if you don't feel confident about doing this, you should not feel obliged. If bottles of wine are placed out for all to share, be careful not to hog them – it's okay to help yourself, but always offer to fill other glasses first – ask 'would you like some wine?'.

If you end up using the wrong glass, don't worry. You'll hardly be shot for it. You can simply ask the waiter for 'another red wine glass' if you need a replacement.

The finer points of dining

Sneezing, coughing and burping
Well, we all do them in the privacy of our own homes, but try not to make a big event out them of when dining out. If you have to, turn your head away from the food, cover your mouth with a clean handkerchief (try not to use your napkin), and get it all over with as quietly and quickly as possible. If you really can't control that terrible cough, say something 'I'm sorry, I'll just go and sort out this cough,' and go outside until the tickle has disappeared.

Awkward items and troublesome food
There are some dishes that are just plain awkward to eat. Anything with small bones, such as fish, needs to be treated with caution. Place the bones on the side of your plate. If by any chance you do get a bone stuck in your throat and really need help, don't let good manners stand in your way. Similarly, if someone else is obviously choking, help them out or ask if anyone can assist.

Any other items that you cannot swallow (pips, stones or pieces of gristle and bone) should be removed from the mouth with as little fuss as possible, perhaps by using your napkin over your mouth, and placed on the side of the place. Do not ever spit anything out enthusiastically and yell 'yuck, a bone!' or similar!

Some food is eaten in a particular way. Caviar, for example, is often served with small, plain biscuits. You put a little caviar on the biscuits with your knife and, depending on the size of the biscuit, you take a bite or pop the whole thing in your mouth. However, if you are dining with people who really know their caviar, there is a different ritual you need to know. You put a little pile of the eggs on the web of skin between the index finger and thumb of your left hand and lick it off. Don't try this unless everyone else is doing it – otherwise you'll get some very funny looks. In fact, don't try it at all unless there's no alternative!

Some foods seem designed to embarrass us at posh occasions. Take garlic, for example. Many of us love the taste, but garlic does leave us with a problem in the fresh-breath department. If everyone else has eaten garlic, that's fine. If it was just you, don't get too up-close-and-personal to other people for a while, or have an after-dinner mint.

Peas are famous for being hard to eat. Technically, the rules of high-class manners say that you are not supposed to turn your fork upside down and use it as a spoon. So use other food on the plate, like potatoes or rice and stick the peas to it. This should avoid the problems of stray peas rolling around your plate as you try to persuade them to go onto your fork.

If in doubt, use your common sense. Most people today are less hung up on the sillier rules of dining, although it always helps to know what they are.

Finger foods

It can be difficult to know just which foods it's okay to pick up in your fingers at a more formal dinner. Watch what other people are doing and copy them. If nobody is picking up their asparagus, you'd probably better not either – even if you know it would be so much easier. Shellfish is usually eaten with the hands, and can be rather messy – usually you'll get some special sharp forks and other tools to help you tackle things like mussels and snails.

Other food just shouldn't be let out in a formal setting. Corn on the cob, for example, is almost impossible to eat politely. Probably best to leave it alone, unless the occasion is an informal barbecue, where everyone is just diving in.

Strange as it may seem, pizza can be another problem when it comes to finger food. At home, we all eat it with our fingers, don't we? Preferably straight out of the pizza-delivery box on a Friday night! But in a restaurant, you would eat a genuine Italian pizza with a knife and fork. It can be a bit of a battle. It may be simplest to cut it into portions and then pick it up in your fingers, and most people will be glad to follow suit – judge the occasion and make your choice.

If nobody is picking up their asparagus, you'd probably better not either – even if you know it would be so much easier.

You can find yourself having the same problem with fruit. At home, you'd crunch straight into that apple, but at a formal occasion you should cut it into pieces and may even want to peel it first. A small, sharp knife is usually provided for this purpose. At a very formal do, you'd use a fork to get the pieces to your mouth. Again, see what everyone else is up to.

The French are especially particular about the correct method to eat cheese. It is not so much the eating that matters, but the way you cut the cheese to begin with. Those produced in round cakes (such as Camembert, for example) are cut by slicing outwards from the centre so that you get a small wedge. That's the best policy with any round cheese, and makes it easier for the next person to serve themselves a similar portion.

Twiddling your noodles

Finally, we need to take a quick look at awkward foods. Pasta, for example, is hugely popular but people are often a little confused about how to handle the long, stringy varieties such as spaghetti and tagliatelle. At a formal dinner you should be given a spoon and fork for this sort of pasta. You pick up a few strands with the fork, hold them against the bowl (the inside surface) of the spoon and wind them around the fork until they form a neat little bundle that you can pop into your mouth. Well, that's the theory! It can take a few goes to get the knack. It's also not such good manners to suck up a string of spaghetti until it pops into your mouth with a 'splat' – not at a formal do, anyway. (And even if it is fun.)

Eating Indian and Chinese food

In Indian and other ethnic restaurants in Britain we use knives and forks as normal. Only if you get invited to a very authentic Asian or Arabic meal will people eat with their fingers, in the traditional manner. Use some rice or bread to help scoop up a ball of food and pop it all into your mouth. Traditionally the left hand is considered 'dirty' by many Eastern cultures, so always use your right hand.

If you are eating Chinese in the west no one will mind if you ask for a spoon or a fork instead of using the chopsticks that are usually provided. If, however, you get invited to a dinner where everyone is eating with chopsticks you might feel foolish if you can't join in. This is one way to do it:

- Take one stick and lay it across your hand so that it rests in the bit between your forefinger and thumb. (If you're right-handed, your right hand).
- Let the end of the stick rest on the inside of your middle finger. This stick does not move.

- Now take the second stick and lay it on top of the first.
- Grasp the second stick between thumb and forefinger. You can now move the stick up and down using it to trap food against the stationary stick. It's easy with a little practice. Incidentally, people from Southeast Asia generally use a spoon and fork and keep chopsticks for eating the noodle course.

In many parts of the world you are expected to eat with noisy enthusiasm (in Japan, for example, slurping appreciatively is quite normal). Watch others and copy what they do. If you insist on western-style good table manners you might look as though you are not enjoying the food – but don't go overboard!

If you are a guest then you have no option but to struggle with difficult food, but if you are the host take pity on your guests and avoid foods that will cause problems. Try to choose foods that are easy to deal with, and won't be regarded as too unusual.

How to eat

Here are a few common-sense suggestions on what makes good manners when eating out in public:

- Eat quietly, taking only small bites at a time.
- Eat with your mouth closed.
- Don't blow on hot food to cool it. Wait until it cools naturally – use the time for conversation.
- What goes into your mouth should not, except in case of dire emergency, come out again. If you have accidentally put something inedible, such as a bone or fruit stone, in your mouth then you should remove it with your fingers as unobtrusively as possible and place it on the side of your plate. Don't spit it out.

Soup

However wonderful it tastes, don't slurp! Old-fashioned rules of etiquette say that it's good manners to eat soup like this: half-fill your spoon (and it is best to aim for a half-full spoon to avoid slurping) by dipping it into your soup and tipping the spoon away from you, so that the soup flows into it. When you get near the end, tip your bowl slightly away from you. That's if you really want to bother with old-fashioned manners, which very few people do. Just eat it quietly, that's all we ask!

- The purpose of a formal meal is to socialise, not to satisfy hunger. Don't ever give the impression that you would rather be eating than talking.
- If you are a naturally fast eater, try to slow it down a bit, so you don't finish before everyone else.
- If you like to chew everything 32 times, try to speed up, so that you won't find everyone else waiting for you to finish.
- If you want to pause, place your knife and fork on the plate, but not together. Only place them together (side by side) if you want to show the waiting staff that you've finished and they can take your plate. Here's an interesting fact: in China, the way to show you have finished your pot of tea and would like some more is to turn the lid upside down on the pot. I've tried this and it works.
- If there is something on the plate you don't like it is quite acceptable just to leave it, or perhaps try a mouthful as a token effort.

After the meal

All the plates are cleared away, and the meal's over – what next? That depends on your hosts really. At some very formal dinners, port or brandy may be brought to the table. At others coffee is served. It used to be the habit that the ladies left the room at this point, leaving the men to their own conversation and cigars – but you wouldn't find that happening today!

The elbow question

The traditional rule used to be 'elbows off the table!', and it was thought rude to lean forward on your elbows while eating. But things have changed, and today it's quite normal to do this, especially if you are dining informally with friends and having a good conversation. But if you're at a very formal occasion and not sure, it's good manners to play safe, until people have obviously relaxed and eating is over. Usually the more formal rules get quickly abandoned once people have got to know each other and are simply having a good time.

If you're seated at a rather cramped table, keep your elbows in and try not to dig other people in the ribs – and hope they'll treat you to the same good manners!

At some formal dinners it is usual to signal the start of the after-meal activities with a loyal toast (that is, toasting the health of the Queen and some members of the royal family). Alternatively, there may be a toast to the person who is being honoured, or simply an announcement that dinner is over and you are welcome to circulate. You are not supposed to smoke before the loyal toast has been drunk. After that you can smoke once invited to do so – but only if the restaurant or venue allows it. If you are a smoker, do think about the other people near you. It may be best to refrain, or to go outside, or into a 'smokers' area.

Speeches

Sitting through after-dinner speeches can be a great pleasure, or a complete bore, depending on how amusing the speaker is (and how sober, in some cases). If you are called upon to give a speech, do make sure you speak up – a common problem is that the speaker is just too quiet for the audience to hear the finer points of the speech.

If you are listening to a speech, stay awake and look interested – even if you would rather be at home clipping your toenails than hearing this old rubbish. It's incredibly bad manners to start talking to your companions, even if they are far more interesting. If the speech contains jokes, laugh a little (even if they're only mildly amusing) and generally help the speaker to feel as if they're doing okay.

Some after-dinner speeches are informative and can be almost like a small lecture. But if questions from the floor are invited, try not to be that annoying person who keeps asking questions when it is quite clear that everyone else wants to get back to their own conversation, even if you harbour a genuine interest in the speaker's subject. Perhaps you'll be able to catch him or her on their own later, or get hold of their card.

In the later stages of a meal it is quite usual for people to move places in order to talk to special friends from whom they have been separated. There are always people who have to leave early to catch trains and so on, so there should be plenty of spare places. At this stage you can be much more informal and talk about things

In the later stages of a meal it is quite usual for people to move places in order to talk to special friends from whom they have been separated.

that interest you and your friends rather than feeling that you have to entertain the people you have been seated with. A chance to relax, at last!

Paying up

If you are eating in a restaurant, rather than simply being an invited guest at a formal banquet, there comes the awful moment when you have to ask for the bill. Asking for the bill is a strange ritual, and one that many of us find quite difficult. The first difficulty is catching the attention of the waiter, who's often really busy getting food to some other diners too, and keeps whizzing by without seeing you. Try to catch the waiter's eye, and if all else fails, do raise your hand a little in the waiter's direction and ask 'could we have the bill, please?' as the waiter passes. If that has no effect, you can always stand up, looking a bit lost – and go and find a waiter to ask if necessary.

Even if the evening out was your idea, your guests may still insist on paying, or in sharing the bill. What you decide with them depends on the situation. It's quite normal today to say 'let's split the bill', so that nobody has to pay for the whole thing. But even if you really want to pay for the whole meal, don't get into a heated 'tussle' if your guests insist on chipping in. Accept graciously and leave it at that. On the other hand, if your companions don't offer to share the cost and the event is not one that you are 'host' for in particular, it's fine to say, in a friendly manner, 'shall we split this?' or 'let's just go halves, shall we?'

Check your bill to see if a service charge has already been added. It may have been, especially if you were dining as part of a large group. In that case it is up to you whether you leave a little extra tip on top, for really outstanding service. Otherwise you will see a notice on the bill that says 'Service not included'. You'll normally see that the final amount on the credit card slip has been left blank so that you can add a gratuity – that's another name for a 'tip'. Traditionally in Britain the usual tip is between 10 and 15 per cent of the bill. So add that amount, or leave it separately as cash – tucked under a plate perhaps. If the service was terrible, well there's no obligation to tip – but it's good manners otherwise.

In much of Europe, you can get coffee and a light snack at a streetside café, served by a waiter, which happens less in Britain. Here the waiter would certainly appreciate a tip, but you only need to leave a small amount, in cash, when you leave.

Drink up!

Drinking usually goes with eating, and alcoholic drinks feature at most social occasions. Alcoholic drinks can help to make the situation more relaxed and enjoyable and can give people confidence and make them more extrovert. In moderation, that can be very helpful in a rather intimidating social situation. And at a banquet or big do, the booze is usually being paid for by someone else, so what could be better? But, even if you are normally a very responsible drinker, do be careful – it's so easy to have one too many and get a bit more than 'tiddly'. And there's not much you can do about it by that point. However shy you may be feeling, it's good manners to keep your drinking well under control, and not to lose too many inhibitions – you may regret it!

Of course every situation is different. At an informal large party with very good friends and family, it may be more acceptable to have a bit too much, get a bit merry and generally behave in a slightly silly way. At a large banquet, in the company of strangers, you would be ill-advised to behave in the same way. One problem

Leaving

Invitations to very formal dinners or events might state
'Carriages at 10.45 pm' which is an old-fashioned way to let
you know when the proceedings will wind up, partly so that
guests can sort out trains and taxis beforehand. It would
have to be a very formal dinner to have actual horse
carriages arrive at the end! Very few formal dinners or
events have leaving formalities, but it is obviously always
good manners to thank your host briefly as you leave. Keep
it simple – remember they have other people to say
goodbye to – and follow up with a thank you letter if you
think it's appropriate. At very formal events there is usually
a member of staff – perhaps a porter or a hotel doorman –
who can call you a taxi, or you can even do it yourself from
the telephone at the hotel reception desk.

is that once we've had a bit too much we tend not to notice how
our behaviour has changed. If you're at all worried, it's best to
keep to soft drinks – there's nothing rude about saying, 'I'm not
drinking tonight' or 'I really would prefer an orange juice,
thanks.' People are likely to think you are driving and simply
being sensible. And of course, you may not ever drink alcohol – if
you don't, either because you don't like it or on principle or for
religious reasons, you can simply politely refuse.

One last important point about getting drunk: getting more
than tiddly is generally a bad idea, and it is extremely bad manners
to get drunk if you are the host of the party. That's because it's
your job to look after everyone and to make sure that all guests are
happy. If you're under the table, you're going to find that difficult.

At a large party, it may also be necessary to make sure there isn't too much noise or rowdy behaviour – you have a duty to remain completely sober, so that things don't get out of hand.

Wine

Some people get in a real tizzy about the ins and outs of wine, and all that expert knowledge that you're, apparently, supposed to know. But really, don't worry about it. All that intimidating language about 'bouquets' and 'a nice nose' is fine, but you don't need it to appreciate a nice glass of wine and enjoy sharing wine with others. Good manners do not hide behind pretentious language, they are found in simple concern for other people's comfort and enjoyment.

But here are a few little tips when it comes to dealing with buying and knowing about wine. Though many of us buy a bottle of wine from the supermarket, you can also buy your wine by the case from a wine merchant – the more expensive and 'classier' wines are sold this way. And in an upmarket restaurant there may well be a wine waiter – a member of staff whose sole job is to help you choose the best wine for your meal. Some wine waiters can be a bit snobby – you can laugh at them, quite justifiably, when you get home, but when you're there it may help you to know at least a little about all the different kinds of wine.

The wine ritual

If you are the host, your wine waiter (called a *sommelier* in the more expensive restaurants – which is just the French word for the same thing) will bring you the wine list to study. If you have someone in your party with a real knowledge of wine you can hand over the job of choosing what you are going to drink to them. However, don't feel you have to. Take the list and study it. You need to know what sort of wine you want. There are no hard-and-fast rules (for example, people used to say you should only drink white wine with fish and poultry, but that's not the case today); you can order what you like. But make sure you know the basics – there are a great many wine guide-type books that can tell you the difference between a chardonnay and a sauvignon, or a pinot noir and a merlot.

When the waiter brings your wine to the table, he will show you the bottle first. You are supposed to read the label and make sure that he's brought the one you ordered. Also have a quick look to check that the capsule (the bit of foil or plastic that seals the top of the bottle) is present and unbroken. It is not unknown in seedier restaurants to sell off leftover wine by putting it into a new bottle. Then the waiter will remove the cork and pour a very small amount of wine into your glass. This is so that you can taste and make sure that it's okay. If you want to do taste the wine thoroughly and 'professionally' you should swill the wine gently in the glass and then stick your nose right in and take a good sniff. But most people feel too self-conscious to do that, and really all that matters is whether the wine is 'corked' or not. If it tastes terrible, a bit like vinegar, it probably is corked – this means that it has reacted chemically with the cork, not that there are bits of cork floating in it. If the wine tastes as if it is corked (and it will usually smell nasty too) tell the waiter, firmly and politely. It's quite in order, and the waiter should replace the bottle without question.

If the wine tastes fine, you don't need to do more than nod at the waiter, or say 'that's fine, thank you.' He will pour a small measure into each glass and then he'll leave the bottle and retire. If you are having white wine, he will put it in some form of cooler and will leave you a cloth so that you can pull it out again without getting wet. By the way, if we're being fussy it is usual with white wine to pick the glass up by the stem rather than the bowl. This is so that your hand does not warm the wine. But it is only important to remember this at parties and wine tastings where you might be holding the glass for some time.

If you are serving the wine yourself, at your own dinner party, obviously you won't want to taste it. You may want to pour a little into your own glass first, in case there are any little fragments of cork in the wine, before serving wine to your guests.

If you are invited to a wine tasting it is polite and practical not to swallow the wine that you are given to taste. You will probably be offered quite a few wines to taste and if you drink them all you'll quite soon be drunk. And that's not the idea! In such surroundings spittoons will be provided and you will be expected to spit the wine out into them – this is one situation where it is good manners to spit in public. You will also be offered small snacks such as little bits of French toast. These are not to keep your hunger at bay, but to clear your palate, so that your tastebuds will be ready for the next wine you taste.

It is usual with white wine to pick the glass up by the stem rather than the bowl. This is so that your hand does not warm the wine.

Incidentally, if you don't drink or don't want to drink any more, it is quite okay to hold your hand over your glass when the wine waiter is doing refills. You don't have to drink another glass. If it is your host who is re-filling, then a few words of explanation ('no more for me, thanks, I'm driving tonight') would be polite. Don't let yourself be pressured into drinking more than you want. Some people may get a bit pushy, because they want to be a 'good host' and can't believe you don't want any more – but they'll understand if you smile and say 'no thanks!'

Champagne

Champagne is a drink for special occasions, for most of us, and it can be difficult to know how to deal with it. We've all seen racing drivers shake up a bottle and splash it all over the podium, but that's not what you should do if you actually want to drink it. Instead, remove the wire retainer around the cork carefully, and put a clean napkin or tea towel over the top of the bottle. Twist and pull the cork carefully, making sure to release the gas pressure gradually. Have a glass ready just in case the wine spurts out a bit. To serve your guests hold the bottle by the bottom. This looks awkward but you'll find it gives you more control than you'd think and it means that you won't warm the bottle with your hand.

There are all sorts of champagnes at a wide range of prices so, as with other wines, it pays to do a bit of research. There are also fizzy wines that are made by the 'champagne method', like cava – they can also be very good, and not quite so expensive. Remember, it is not always the most expensive wine that tastes best. Look out for champagne-style wines from countries you might not expect, such as Australia and New Zealand, or Spain.

Fine wines

Very old, fine wines are likely to have quite a bit of sediment in the bottom. After all, they've been around for a while. If you are serving a wine like this, it's best to decant it – transfer it to a decanter – well before the dinner. There's a traditional trick to spotting the sediment – you are supposed to put a lighted candle behind the bottle to help you spot any that might escape into the decanter. If you feel that it is safe to serve the wine straight from the bottle, it is usual to leave the bottle open for some hours before the wine is served. This gives it a chance to 'breathe'. Even a less expensive red wine can benefit from being opened a little earlier.

Spirits

The Scots/Scandinavian custom of drinking spirits as a beer chaser is becoming increasingly popular, and carries the risk that you will get very drunk very quickly. Schnapps is often drunk cold, with the effect that the alcohol doesn't take effect immediately – so you may not realise how strong it is for quite a few minutes.

Whisky is an equally potent spirit. Most popular brands are blends of several different malts. But more expensive whiskies are single malts – which means that they are not blended. Savour them as you would a good glass of wine – they're expensive, but worth it.

Brandy is another drink that needs to be savoured rather than swigged. The balloon-shaped glass allows you to swirl it around and warm it with your hand, releasing a delicious bouquet and making the spirit less fiery to drink. When it is really warm it should slide over your tastebuds like silk – a very nice sensation indeed!

Pub customs

For some people the British custom of buying a round in a pub is confusing, because it isn't done in all countries. In many places everyone buys their own drinks, and only buys other drinks for close friends and family. This isn't seen as rude at all. So if a visitor doesn't offer to buy a round in the pub, they are not necessarily being bad-mannered, they just don't understand British ways. Part of the reason that buying a round is popular is to take the aggro out of getting the drinks in. It's far less inconvenient if one person takes on the chore, and everyone takes turns. But if you are buying a lot of drinks there's no reason you shouldn't ask to 'share the round' with someone else.

Going to stay

Being the perfect guest – or the perfect host

Know your limits

Being invited to stay with someone opens up a whole range of possible 'foot in mouth' situations, but these can easily be avoided if you're well prepared. The main thing to remember is that when you go to stay with someone you're going to be 'invading their space' while you're there and you need to be sensitive to this, so that you don't get on their nerves. However much they are looking forward to your visit, even the best of friends can find guests a bit stressful at times – and you don't want to ruin a friendship.

First of all, get an idea of how long the visit is supposed to be – if they've said 'come for the weekend', then it's obvious. But if someone says 'do come and stay, for as long as you like,' you need to think about how long that really means. It may need a bit of flexibility on your behalf – often you can't really tell how long to stay until you get there. But, be certain – 'as long as you like' doesn't mean, 'for months on end'!

Don't expect too much

It's easy to get very excited about visiting someone, or having someone to stay with you. With everyone wanting everything to be 'just perfect', it's likely that the visit is likely to feel slightly disappointing – you, as host or guest, were probably just expecting too much. And remember, if everyone feels that they've got to make the visit perfect, they'll be under a terrible strain from the word go. And even the most well-prepared host is probably going to crack under the strain of looking after guests for 24 hours a day, for several days on end. As a guest, the effort of being 'on your best behaviour' for such a long time isn't going to be easy either. Really, it's best if everyone just tries to relax and have a good time. If you're the host, remember that guests don't require looking after all the time and might even like some time alone to read the paper or just hang about doing nothing. Having good manners with regard to your guests doesn't mean that you have to run after them all the time. And, as a guest, your good manners will make you sensitive to the host's need to put their feet up for a while, and have a bit of private 'breathing room' without worrying if you're okay all the time. And, remember, if little things go wrong, or a few stressed-out words get said, just ignore them. However much you enjoy having guests, being 'on guest alert' all the time can leave you a little exhausted!

On the other hand, if the visit does seem to be going very badly, take your cue as a guest to tactfully bring it to an end – find a sudden work commitment or a family problem that requires you leave, perhaps. A few white lies are better than staying in a situation where both host and guests are extremely unhappy. But be good-mannered about it, and depart on as friendly terms as you can manage.

Making a good impression

As a guest, you should arrive bearing gifts for your hosts. If you're simply coming to stay for a couple of days, something simple is fine – perhaps a bottle of wine, or some flowers and chocolates. If you're coming for rather longer, you could bring something a little more grand – toys that would appeal to any of the family's children are a good choice (but make sure you have brought something for all the children, or something they can share). But if you are not extremely well off, don't worry too much – you can also ask your hosts in advance 'is there anything I can bring?' or 'shall I bring some starters for dinner?', giving you a chance to bring some home-made food or something simpler.

Once you've arrived, do make sure that you show interest in all the family – including the kids, and even the family pets. If you're not too used to talking with children, just asking what they did at school today, or to show you their favourite toy, is a good opener.

If you're the host, remember that guests don't require looking after all the time, and might even like some time alone

And don't forget that many small children find adults a bit 'scary', so don't think they are being rude if they run off to mum or dad! Whatever you do, try not to find yourself saying 'how much you've grown!' to the kids themselves – it won't do much for your street cred. If there are dogs or cats, or other pets, do stroke or greet them if you are comfortable with that. Conversely, if you are a host with pets, be considerate to the fact that not all guests are thrilled when Rover jumps up to say hello.

Above all, it's good manners to take everyone as they come. You may be spending time with people different from you, with different kinds of jobs or lifestyles. Don't be judgemental, be interested. You never know how well you might get on with someone who has a very different kind of life from yours.

Play by the house rules

When you stay with someone, you have to fit in with the way they live their lives – and that can bit a bit hard. Even if people's habits, like meal times or when they go to bed, are very unlike yours, you'll need to do the same. If a family follows little observances you're not used to – like saying grace at a meal – simply accept it. If you say grace, but your guests don't, live with it rather than complain. If you're the host, bear in mind that your guests may also have little quirks that you can easily accommodate, if you take the trouble to ask – for instance, a guest might be used to making themselves a hot drink if they can't sleep, or getting up early to go for a run. Show them where the hot chocolate or the breakfast cereal is, and ask them to make themselves at home.

Mainly, for both guest and host, remember that it's good manners to say in advance if there is something you would appreciate, like a hot water bottle in bed perhaps, or some family ritual, like letting mum have the shower first because she has to get to work, that your guest needs to know.

Make space and time for your guests

As already mentioned, everyone needs time for themselves occasionally, some more than others. If you're the host, make sure that you have provided space in the day for your guest to relax. Don't crowd them all the time. If your guest is not used to the hustle and bustle of family life and yours is a very hustle-bustle family with lots of kids and dogs, try to keep the kids away a bit, some of the time. Look out for signs that your guest is a little overwhelmed by it all.

Know when to say nothing

For guests, this next bit of 'good manners' advice is obvious really, but even so, many of us are guilty of falling at the first hurdle on this one. You are the guest – so, not a word of criticism about your friends' way of life. Don't wander around saying 'hmm, wouldn't have gone for this wallpaper myself' or 'gosh, don't you ever discipline your children, they really are out of control.' This is just as true if you are visiting relatives and a lot of really big family rows start just because one person has decided to give their opinion on how their relative chooses to run their life. However much temptation beckons, keep your opinions unspoken.

Remember that your host is letting you into their private domain, and they are letting you share all the things they value most in their life. So don't hurt them with insensitive remarks. Ignore the décor that makes you, personally, feel a bit ill. Perhaps they'd hate your place just as much. If their kids seem a noisy lot, and yours are little angels, feel glad – but don't go on about it. Just be happy to share the company and hospitality of friends. This holds just as much if you're the host – just smile, and laugh about it later if you have to.

Keep it friendly
Same thing applies here, when you're conversing with your hosts. If you keep the conversation light and friendly, you should be able to steer clear of any contentious areas, where you and your hosts might violently disagree. Even so, you are likely to have some longer and more serious conversations, if you're staying for a while. You may end up watching the TV news together or reading the newspapers, so topics of the day are likely to come up. Well, if you know your hosts even slightly – and most likely you will – you'll have an idea of the political opinions they're likely to hold, and what they may feel about news items. So avoid areas where you are likely to conflict, or at least keep it tactful. And don't assume that everyone holds the same views as you – it's an easy mistake to make. Even friends you've known for some time can surprise you.

Religion can be a very hot topic, and if you hold very different religious views from your hosts (or guests, according to which you are), or have no religious belief, while they do, it may be best to keep away from the subject if you can. If religion comes up in conversation be non-committal or open-minded, and don't get into a deep discussion. If a topic comes up that you really feel strongly about, and fear will start a raging argument, the best thing may be to say 'well, let's not talk about that – it'll only get me over-excited' or some other such tactful way of stopping a row from starting. If necessary, find a sudden need to go to the toilet, and hope that the subject will have changed by the time you return!

Clear up

If you're a guest, remember that you need to respect your hosts' home and keep it tidy, even if you are a complete slob in the privacy of your own place. So, when you get up in the morning, make the bed and tidy up your room. If you have books or papers out, clear them up. Mess can really get on some people's nerves, so be sensitive to that, even if you personally don't mind mess a bit. It also works the other way – if you're a very untidy host, with a neat and natty guest, you may stress them out completely if you don't clear up some of those books, clothes or piles of CDs. It doesn't have to be a palace – just a bit of a clear-up helps.

Lend a hand

As a guest at someone else's house you should offer to help 'make yourself useful' often. Offer to lay the table, do the washing-up, or pop to the shops for any food items needed. Most hosts are grateful for a bit of assistance when they've got guests, even if they initially say 'oh no, don't bother!'. Ask again, and only sit down and do nothing if you're completely sure if they don't want you to help at all. Hosts – it's not bad manners to let your guests help out a bit, and don't be ungracious if someone offers to wash up or some other useful chore. Smile and say 'thanks'.

Don't make yourself too much at home

When you go to stay with people they will often say 'treat the place as your own', as a way of inviting you to relax. But don't do that literally – it would be very bad manners to use their things without asking, or help yourself to the contents of the fridge. Another complete no-no is using the telephone all the time, and running up expensive bills. And don't invite your friends to phone you there non-stop either – that's just as rude. If you'd like to use the phone, ask – and if it's long-distance, insist on paying for the call.

In general, fit in with the 'rhythm of life' at your friend's house. If they go to bed early, follow suit – don't force them to stay up late, just to be polite, when they're obviously tired and used to getting a good eight hours' sleep each night. Just try to read the situation – Saturday night may be fine to stay up into the early hours chatting, but on Sunday night they may have work the next day. Good manners here are just a common-sense thing.

If you're particularly old friends with one of your hosts, you may have a wealth of stories about silly and embarrassing things they did in their youth, or with other partners. Don't tell these stories unless you're absolutely sure your friend won't mind – there may be some his or her partner, or kids, just don't know. And they may want to keep it that way. Don't be the guest who caused red faces all round.

And so to bed

Things can get a little awkward here. If you're a guest who came with a friend, your host may not be quite sure whether you sleep together or not. Help your host out – it's good manners to make the nature of your relationship quite clear early on, so that everyone is comfortable with what's what. Just drop it into the conversation if you can, ideally when the invitation is issued, although you can do it once you've arrived. 'Steve's my partner' or 'Jane's my girlfriend' are often sufficient. Or, you may prefer to have a quiet word with your host – 'so Jane and I are quite happy bunking up together, no need for separate rooms' – if it seems confusion might arise. Bear in mind that older relatives, or people with strict religious views, may decide to provide separate rooms – don't take offence, it's their home after all. Just grin and bear it. You won't be there forever.

As a host, don't be afraid to tactfully ask, if the situation doesn't seem clear. You can say something like 'John, I've put you and Steve together, hope I've got that right – plenty of room though if you want to go separately', or you can just ask outright. Usually the situation is fairly clear from early on in the visit.

What guests should do

It's good manners to show that you are appreciative of your host's hospitality and that you're enjoying yourself. But you can't go around saying 'thank you' all the time. Instead, admire the home, or say approving things about the garden or the children. Show interest in your hosts' hobbies. Generally make them

In general, fit in with the 'rhythm of life' at your friend's house.

happy by showing them your pleasure in their life and family, and also do take time occasionally to say 'thank you so much for inviting me, I'm very much enjoying being with you and your family' or something similar. If you are feeling generous, you could show your thanks by offering to take them out for a meal.

Or if you're a great cook, you could offer to cook breakfast one morning. When you leave, you should buy your hosts a little present. Having got to know them better, you probably have an idea of something they might especially like – 'Jack, I thought you might like a couple of new books on fishing to add to the collection', or something that all the family might enjoy eating or drinking (after you've gone!). And don't forget to follow up with a thank-you note, especially if the visit was during a holiday season and your hosts had gone to a great deal of trouble. Last but not least – if it's appropriate, perhaps you can invite them to stay with you some time?

Gracious hospitality

What the host should do

Here is a bit of advice on being a good host, and making your guests feel at ease. Do give your guests a short guided tour of the house, so that they know where the bathrooms and loos are, and where they will be sleeping. If there are any strange quirks – a door that's likely to stick, or a window that is a bit fragile – try to mention them early on: 'I'd watch that bathroom door, it has fallen off the hinges when I've yanked it too hard, once or twice' or 'now, just to say be careful with the window in your room, and you need to unlock it with this key.'

Think about little luxuries that might make the stay more pleasant for your guest. Perhaps a TV in their room, or tea and coffee things and a kettle?

Sometimes we get so used to 'working' our home that we forget about all those funny little bits and pieces, or that step that everyone else seems to fall over.

Think about little luxuries that might make the stay more pleasant for your guest. Perhaps a TV in their room, or tea and coffee things and a small kettle? It will help them to feel more at home and would mean they don't always have to ask. Make sure they have some books and magazines in their room, and – if you have spares – a dressing gown or robe. And don't forget to provide bath towels and any other necessities. Say something like 'now, just ask if there's anything you need', and most people will let you know if they need something like a glass for some water, or some tissues, or whatever. No guest will expect you to offer the swanky luxuries of a hotel (well, no polite and well-mannered guest will!) but a little pampering goes a long way.

Getting around

Many of us spend quite a bit of our time travelling – for work, for pleasure, to get from A to B. And there's no two ways about it: despite the glut of budget airlines, the faster trains, and the many different ways we can travel nowadays, we still have to put up with delays, overcrowding and other annoyances. Sometimes it seems as if travel is no fun at all, especially when you're stuck in a traffic jam. Sometimes travel is exhilarating, but sometimes it's boring, frustrating, claustrophobic, noisy and dirty. It's quite easy to get stressed out by it all and to take it out on our fellow travellers. So, bear in mind that good manners are an essential when it comes to getting through our tricky travel moments.

So, let's start with an obvious point of 'travel manners': when is it good manners to give up your seat to someone else? In days of yore, a gentleman or a boy would always offer their seat to a lady, no matter how old or young. That's no longer true. Today people are treated more equally and a woman might even find this a little annoying. But, common-sense good manners say that you should offer your seat to anyone who seems more in need of it than you – a pregnant woman, an older man or woman, someone who is disabled, someone with young children in tow. It doesn't matter whether you are a man or a woman, anyone who needs a seat will be grateful of the offer. If they choose not to take it, at least you've offered. If they have the bad manners to appear cross about it, then take it in your stride – although that's a rare occurrence.

In general, don't take your travel frustrations out on employees of the travel company, who can't possibly be directly responsible for the fact that your train's delayed, or your flight has been cancelled. It's good manners to be civil and as pleasant as you can be – although of course you can tell them that you are unhappy about a situation and be firm in insisting that they help you to resolve any difficulties that have arisen as a result. Don't bully or hector staff – bad manners and also not very effective!

Don't rage on those roads

It's hard not to get cross, isn't it, when that idiot in the other car has come just 'that near' your bumper and has then flashed his headlights to try and intimidate you further. Not much you can do except keep a wary eye on him and make sure nothing that you are doing is likely to upset other drivers unnecessarily. Angry drivers are dangerous drivers, apart from anything else. So here are a few tips on driving behaviour to avoid, things that police and motoring organisations like the AA always say are designed to wind up other motorists:

- Be polite, and don't get too close to the car in front. This kind of 'tailgating' is rude and dangerous if the person ahead needs to stop suddenly.
- Don't cut up other drivers. 'Nipping in' in front of someone can be very aggravating and doesn't really save you much time.
- Don't stick in the middle lane of the motorway. It's supposed to be for overtaking only.
- Don't beep the car horn to express anger or frustration: it's only there to signal danger and caution. Behave, now!
- Always try to indicate well in advance. It can be easy to forget to indicate if you know a route well, or are lost and turning suddenly. Think about the person behind.

Of course these are just a few hints on sensible, safe driving. Here are a couple of common-sense tips that are to do with good manners on the road: if you're in a heavy, slow-moving stream of traffic and people are waiting to get on, be considerate and make room if possible. And when you're parking, don't just leave your car anywhere, or straddled over two spaces or blocking an entrance.

And for goodness sake, don't make a fuss if cars choose to park outside your house at the curb. They have every right to, as long as the road allows parking and they're not blocking your drive. However much you might prefer to have an unobstructed car-free view, you can't decide where people can or cannot park. Sorry!

Get on your bike!

Cyclists occupy a strange position – not exactly a vehicle, but not a pedestrian. When surrounded by motor vehicles, cyclists are vulnerable and when surrounded by pedestrians they can be dangerous. So good travel manners are particularly important here. Cycling without thought for others is rude because it can cause harm to pedestrians and alarm to motorists. Besides, if you get knocked off your bike by a driver, you are far likely to come off worst. However much you hate cars, as a cyclist you have to respect the rules of the road and also respect that you may be virtually invisible to some less observant drivers.

As a cyclist, it may seem easier to ride along the pavement with the pedestrians, but that's a rather impolite way of cycling, and you could easily injure someone who wasn't expecting you to come along. If you do end up cycling on what is really a footpath, be careful – keep your distance from pedestrians and ring your bell when need be. But don't ring your bike bell loudly and frantically if you want to get through a crowd of pedestrians – just get off and walk.

When cycling on the road, make sure that you're wearing appropriate clothing, especially at night or in bad weather. And use lights. Always give clear signals, to indicate to motorists what you're about to do (and never give rude hand signals, however clear they may be!). Even if you are a very adept cyclist, it really isn't good manners to dash across traffic or make sudden manoeuvres, just to get to make a turn. If you're stuck, get off the bicycle and walk across the crossroads at the lights with the pedestrians – there's no shame in it, after all!

If you're part of a cycling group, it's very bad road manners to cycle in a spread-out and rambling mess. You should always cycle in single file, leaving plenty of room for cars to pass. Never block the road, unintentionally or otherwise. Lastly, don't park your bike just anywhere – make sure it isn't blocking a pavement or footpath and always make sure that it is okay to lock it up where you've chosen.

The horse brigade

There's something very nice about seeing someone riding their horse along a country lane, but a bit of common-sense good horse manners is needed to avoid problems. For a start, horses are not machines – they're animals that can at any moment act unpredictably, especially if something suddenly frightens them or startles them from their happy trotting. A rearing, lunging horse is a sight to behold and not one you particularly want to behold through your car windscreen, either. If you are the rider, make sure that you know how to control your horse before you take it out on the public highway, for everyone's safety.

When riding, it's good manners to keep your distance from people on foot. Also, just because you don't have flashing indicators doesn't mean you shouldn't give any warning of where you're going. Give clear indications and also wear high-visibility clothing – and a riding hat, of course.

If you're driving past someone on a horse, give them a wide berth and slow down, well before you reach them, to give the horse some warning. As a rider, wave or smile to thank the passing motorist and if the road is narrow, it can help to give the driver behind you an indication of when it's safe to pass you.

I'm on the train…

It's not just people shouting loudly on their mobile phones that annoys train passengers. Here are a few things that can really get up people's noses, quite rightly too:

- Leaving luggage in the aisles, or on the seat beside you, even though the train is full.
- Putting your feet up on the seat in front of you, especially when the train is crowded.
- Taking up all the leg room so that other people have to sit in a cramped position.
- Insisting on having the window open or closed when it clearly bothers everyone else.
- Using the sort of headphones that let the sound escape. No one wants to listen to a couple of hours of tinny percussion while sitting next to you. Really.
- Forcing your company on people who would rather not talk.
- And of course, treating everyone to a free listen to your phone conversation.

That list is pretty obvious really, isn't it? Except perhaps for the one about talking to people who aren't interested in having a conversation. Some people just hate chatting to strangers, or have other things they want to do – like read, or do some work, or just enjoy looking out of the window at the scenery passing by. So, be considerate. Even if you personally can't think of anything better than chatting to your neighbour to fill the time, make sure that the feeling's mutual. A friendly smile and a polite remark (often involving that old British favourite, the weather) will usually help you to 'test the water'. If your companion seems encouraging, you can expand the scope of your conversation. If you get a brief or even chilly response you will know better than to force the issue.

Going underground

The London Underground, known to all Londoners as 'The Tube', is a great place to get really annoyed, especially when the train is hot, packed, and late again. A real test of good manners! A few reminders, here:

- Just because you have been pushed into a position where your face is six inches from the person next to you, it doesn't mean you are now best friends. If you catch someone's eye, perhaps a quick sympathetic grimace is okay, but starting a long chat isn't going to be appreciated by most people, who'd rather pretend they were the only person on the train and get the journey over with.
- When the Tube train pulls into the station, do wait until everyone who's getting off has, before getting on.
- If you have a rucksack on, take it off when you get on the train. It's so easy to forget you are wearing it, and bash half the other passengers behind you.
- Don't hold the doors open to prevent the train leaving; it just delays the train and can be very dangerous.

- Don't block the escalators. On the London Tube it's the custom to stand on the right (keeping your luggage in front of you) and let people in a hurry run up or down the left-hand side. People in London are always in a hurry and rather short on patience, so if you block the escalator, they will try to push past you and this is potentially dangerous.
- If you're really lost people will usually give you directions, but do try to use the plentiful maps and diagrams first, and you can also approach uniformed station staff.

Move along the bus, please!

Most of the things that apply to the Tube also apply to travel by bus or coach. There is always a place to store luggage and baby buggies, so use it and don't leave them blocking the aisle or occupying seats. Pushing and shoving to get on or off will also make you unpopular.

Sometimes it is hard to gauge where the front of the queue starts, especially when there is a large crowd of people waiting for the bus. But there *is* a queue, however ramshackle it may seem – so don't be tempted to try and push into the front, or side, when the bus arrives. You'll only get some very cross looks.

When travelling by bus try to have the right change for the fare – it will speed up the boarding process and will make the driver happy. For many bus services you can also buy tickets in advance – in London from streetside machines, Tube stations and many newsagents. That can make things run much more smoothly, and is likely to make your driver (and you) much more happy. Handing a £10 note over to the driver for a 50p fare is not going to make him or her too pleased.

Up in the air

Air travel has its own unique stresses. For a start, delays are common at the airport and you just have to try to stay calm and take it in your stride. Yelling at airport staff doesn't really do much to help the issue, or endear you to your fellow passengers. Play nice, and be as good-tempered as you can, even if you are feeling tired and dejected, with three even more tired and dejected kids in tow.

Today you can often book your seat on a scheduled flight ahead of time – even when you buy your ticket. Even so, the nicer seats are often gone and you may not get the window or aisle seat you'd hoped for. If that matters a lot to you, try and get there very early so that you are more likely to be successful, especially if you are a family group. The budget airlines sometimes offer flights where the seats are not allocated and it's just a case of getting on and picking a seat. However much you want it, it's not good manners to fight over the last remaining window seat, okay?!

Taking a great deal of hand luggage is unlikely to win you friends and may cost you money. Once on the plane, the worst thing about economy air travel is the cramped conditions. You'll have to be considerate of those around you – don't kick the back of the seat in front, elbow your neighbour or hog the armrest. When you recline your seat, be aware of the person behind you. It's simple consideration in the face of awful conditions that makes for good air-travel manners!

Children can be very annoying to other passengers in a plane, because there is little they can do to escape rowdy or over-excited kids, however much they'd love them in normal circumstances. If you have kids with you, watch that they aren't annoying fellow passengers by running around, or banging the seat backs or trays. It may seem like nothing much to you, and at least it's keeping them occupied. But the person next door may already be exhausted and just longing for some quiet. It's a good idea to come well prepared with toys and simple games to keep your children occupied – colouring books and jigsaw puzzles, or some new comics or books. On the other hand, if you're the one who's scowling at your neighbours' noisy kids, do remember that for most children the flight is a very exciting adventure, and a quick game of peek-a-boo from behind the headrest might be all you need to do to keep the youngster amused for a few minutes.

However much you want it, it's not good manners to fight over the last remaining window seat.

As with train journeys, and perhaps more so, don't assume that the person next to you wants to spend the journey chatting to you. Everyone's different, and while you may be an interested extrovert, other people just want to curl up and go to sleep and try to forget that their cramped legs have already gone to sleep some time ago. Try to take the hint if someone smiles, says a few words, and then gets back to their book.

Ship ahoy!

Going on a cruise? The nearest most of us get to life at sea is a cross-Channel ferry or, at best, a tourist cruise. Both of these are really no more than a floating train, or a floating hotel, respectively. There are no special rules, except that on the grander cruises you might be asked to 'dress for dinner' – that is, wear smart cocktail or evening wear. In that case, you'll have been given full details beforehand, when you booked. But today there are no particular manners that you need to observe. Even the captain – who used to have to 'go down with the ship' if it sunk – is allowed to get into the lifeboat with everyone else these days! About the only thing that might happen is that, on a cruise, you can be asked if you'd like to dine at the captain's table – treat this as a formal dinner and you'll have a good idea of how to behave and dress.

By the way, it is a myth that the captain of a ship can perform marriage ceremonies, so don't ask!

Communications

Today we can pick up the phone, send an instant message, text a message, tap out an email, even set up a webcam and send live pictures. Or even if we don't know how to do all of those, you can bet our younger relatives probably can. It's hard to imagine how people survived, in the not-too-distant past, when writing was the main form of communication over a distance, later to be followed by those new-fangled gadgets like the telegraph and telephone. Digital technology and especially the internet, of course, has been responsible for much of this huge expansion of communication, which affects our world in every aspect, not least our informal communication with each other. And with new forms of communication come new ideas of what is polite and what isn't – what makes good communication 'manners'. Indeed, the 'rules' of how to communicate politely on the internet even have a tongue-in-cheek word that people use for them – 'netiquette'. If you are diving into internet communication and email for the first time, there are a few points that might help you feel less worried about the whole experience.

Email
Those of us who maybe only use email for the occasional message might be surprised to realise that it is probably the most widely used form of communication in the world. Even developing nations are now gaining more access to email. It's an amazing way to communicate with people who may be thousands of miles away from you, and to send them documents, pictures or even music

electronically. You can send a whole book at the touch of a button. And, with a few clicks of the mouse, you can send your message to as many people as you want, or as few.

The advantages of email are obvious. However, one of the big disadvantages is that it's hard to make them as personal or obviously friendly as a letter in your own handwriting, or a tone of voice down a telephone. So don't assume that someone is being rude if their message seems terse or cool, it is probably 'just the email talking'.

An email from a work colleague, or from somebody emailing in a work-related capacity, might come across quite like a letter, even if it is brief:

> Andrew
>
> Do you think you could bring that spare case of widgets over when you make the delivery on Wednesday?
>
> Stephen
>
> Stephen Pearce
> Area Sales Manager
> Grummet & Widget International plc
> www.grummetnwidget.com
>
>
> This email and any files transmitted with it are confidential and intended solely for the use of the individual or entity to whom they are addressed. If you have received this email in error please notify the system manager.

However, there's no real need to imitate a formal letter, like that. More often you can be more informal; you can start your message with 'Dear…' or even a simple 'Hello' or 'Hi'.

Hi Andrew,
Could you bring over that box of widgets next time?
Thanks so much,
Stephen

On the whole, the tone and content of an email is more likely to work if you keep to the same format you would use in a phone conversation with the person you're emailing.

Partly because computers used to be much slower, and longer emails took more 'effort' to send, a system of abbreviations developed, to make messages shorter. Someone might write 'AFAIK' instead of 'As Far As I Know'. This soon became quite a trend, and today lots of people use abbreviations as a kind of clever, jokey way of making messages more informal. You certainly don't have to use them, but you may see some, like 'BTW' – 'by the way', or 'IMV' – 'in my view'. If you search for "Internet Lingo" on Google (another internet success story that everyone uses all the time) you're bound to find some information on others. Some of the abbreviations are formal, simple shortcuts, others are intentionally funny, like ROTFLOL – 'rolling on the floor laughing out loud!', in response to a joke

In addition, many people use strange little signs, made up of punctuation marks, which have come to be called 'emoticons'. They're yet another way that people try to make email seem more informal. Two of the most familiar are the smiley face – :-) and the wink – ;-). If you don't get it, turn this page around 90 degrees and look at the page again! Today, many email programs are very clever and if people type one of the well-known emoticons, the program translates it visually into a little yellow smiley face – the right way up as well.

:-)	smiley face (humour)
:-))	laugh
;-)	wink (light sarcasm)
:-|	indifference
:->	devilish grin (heavy sarcasm)
8-)	big-eyed smiley
:-D	shock or surprise
:-(	sad
:-C	really unhappy
:-P	wry smile
;-}	leer
:-X	big wet kiss
:-O	yell

It may all seem very silly to you, but it's simply a kind of optional internet humour, used not only by 'geeks' – those folks who just love computers – but many internet users.

When you write an email it's entirely up to you whether you use lingo and emoticons. People won't expect them. However, there are a few general rules of good manners in email that people have come to expect:

- Don't write in capitals. This is known as 'shouting' and is considered to be VERY RUDE.
- If you are replying to someone's message, or if you are reply to a message on a newsgroup or other email bulletin board that you may be on, always 'quote' the message when you reply. That is, have your program set up so that the original message is quoted as part of your reply. Your email program should do this automatically: if it doesn't you need to go to the 'preferences' part of the program, or

similar, and 'turn on quoting'. It's considered a bit rude to reply like this:

> Hi Mark,
> Yes, that would be fine.
> All the best,
> Jennifer.

Why? Well, busy Mark may have sent out several messages, and received quite a few back – he can't necessarily remember what on earth you're talking about. This is far better:

> Hi Mark
> Mark Battley wrote:
> >Can I come over on Tuesday at 10am to fix that pipe
> that's leaking?
> Yes, that would be fine.
> All the best,
> Jennifer.

- Think before you send – and never send in ire! Sending very angry or rude responses to an email is known as 'flaming' and people find it very rude, especially if you do it to a group or 'list' that you are on. Remember how hard it is to convey emotion in an email – your irate message may sound much more offensive than you intend. Always calm down before you respond and read through the message before you send it – because you won't be able to get it back.
- Don't email any message that you wouldn't mind the world reading. Because no message is completely private:

messages can end up stored on backup servers, saved on hard drives, or sent to the wrong person. A private message might be sent on to a whole crowd of your work colleagues, intentionally or by mistake. Always use discretion. Imagine you are on the phone in a public place – sending email is a little like that.

- It's especially important to think about how you want to come across in a business email. Don't be too jokey and informal if this is a business relationship where you need to keep the usual professional distance. You may find it hard to be more formal with the person 'in the flesh' if you have sent them lots of silly messages.
- Sometimes you will accidentally end up with information, such as the email addresses of other people, that has been sent in error. It is, of course, polite to delete this information and on no account should you make any use of it.

The internet

The internet is an amazing way for people to communicate in real time. Not only can we find out amazing amounts of useful (and not so useful!) information, with search engines like Google, but we can 'talk' to our friends, and people we may never have met, in real time. Instant messaging and chat rooms abound on the internet – there are chat rooms for almost every human interest, from archery to zoo-keeping. This little book can't explain the ins and outs here, but there will be many resources in your local computer book shop, or on the internet itself.

Chat-room 'good manners' differs, depending on the chat room. In some you have to ask to 'enter', in others you can simply join in the discussion as soon as you start, or 'log on'. You usually have the option to remain anonymous if you want, and that isn't considered rude. Someone who joins an email list, or a live chat group, and remains an interested observer rather than joining in is called a 'lurker'. Contrary to how it sounds, this isn't rude at all! It just means someone who isn't an active participant in the discussion – and that's perfectly okay, although other members of the group may be pleased if you 'de-lurk' and introduce yourself eventually.

Many chat rooms and email lists have a 'moderator'; this is someone who has voluntarily taken on the role of looking after the list and making sure there is no rude or aggressive behaviour. Someone can be barred from a list if they 'flame' abuse, or keep writing messages that are 'off topic' – that is, not related to the subject that the list or chat room supports. Anyone sending spam, electronic junk mail in the form of adverts and promotional emails, will be barred almost immediately from well-run groups.

Lastly, a word of advice on internet communication – be careful out there! There are lots of people who are not necessarily who they say they are and you should act as cautiously as you would with a stranger who knocks on your front door. It is quite polite to go only by your first name, and it is sensible internet security to NEVER put your home address and phone number in your personal email messages. Many people make the mistake of doing this, and end up with a lot of junk mail – or even suffering identity fraud – as a result.

Making a call

The phone has become second nature to us now. Most of us have at least one telephone in our home and may also have a mobile as well, or instead. We're used to being completely informal and chatty on the phone, as well as using it for communicating serious or informative matters. Few of us need help in knowing how to use one, but there are a few hints on good phone manners that can help smooth a conversation.

If you call someone, and it is not a completely informal call to family or friends, it helps to announce who you are and, if the person who answers is not who you wish to speak to, to ask for that person by name:

"Hello, this is Sophie Price. Is Janey Griggs there?"

If the person who answers says that no, she isn't there, ask 'may I leave her a message please?' (if you want to) or politely finish the conversation. It's common sense really, but so often we forget to say who we are, what we want, or to thank the person who bothered to pick up the phone in the first place (and may have put down a pile of books, hurried across the office, and be rather puffed out by now, just to pick up the phone for you).

And, think about the time of day you phone. It's so easy to pick up the phone and call, day or night, but do remember that it is rude to call early in the morning, or late at night, or at mealtimes. Try to avoid these times unless it's a real emergency, or you know that the person really doesn't mind. If you do have to phone at an awkward time, apologise and also ask 'is this a convenient time to talk?' You can offer to call back at a mutually convenient time if possible.

Today, many people have answerphones or voicemail services. Don't be intimidated by these. Some of us dry up as soon as we hear the beep, after which we are supposed to leave a message. Remember that the message will be recorded. If you are unsure of what to say, simply leave your name and your telephone number. Do speak clearly and loudly enough to be heard; there's nothing worse than a garbled message where the number to call is inaudible. If you're worried, you can always call back again later, or call back and record a message once you have it written down.

A golden rule of good manners on the phone is: don't forget

that you are talking to another human being, and treat them with the respect you'd want from them. Sometimes it can be easy to feel that the call you are making, perhaps to a customer service centre miles away, is completely anonymous, but it isn't. Don't take out your frustrations with some company's insanely aggravating automated system on the first poor human being you happen to get put through to. If it helps, swear at the 'hold music', and save your good manners for the person who comes on the line.

Mobile phones

Most of us have a real love-hate relationship with mobile phones. For some people they are as important and ordinary as the bunch of keys in their pocket, or the credit cards in their wallet. Mobile phones have revolutionised the way we communicate – now we can phone just about anywhere from just about anywhere. The trouble is that many of us do that!

It sometimes seems as if mobile phones bring out the rudeness in people, but really it's just a lack of consideration. Once you're on the phone, it's easy to forget about everyone else around you, and who is listening in – not by choice – to you telling your friend all about what you did last night. Although some people would love to ban mobile phones from all public areas, that's pretty unrealistic – but it is possible to use a mobile phone in a way that doesn't disrupt everyone else's life. Keep your voice down, and remember the people around you.

Always turn your phone off in places where the ringing could disturb others. In most cinemas, theatres and concert halls you are warned that mobiles are to be turned off. And you usually aren't allowed to use mobiles in hospitals, or during takeoff and landing in a plane, when the mobile could interfere with equipment on the aircraft. But show good 'mobile manners' and think about turning your phone off at other times – if you're in a place where it would be difficult to take a call quietly, for instance. Also, if you have the option, set your mobile to ring on 'vibrate' – far less intrusive than a loud ringtone, however much you, personally, like it.

Thumbs up

Mobile phones can also be used to send text messages – even if you don't use your phone for that, you've probably seen people using a thumb to tap out messages, which they then send to friends. Texting has its own shorthand, with thumb-efficient abbreviations like: 'Hi m8! How U? Me OK. Meet 4 cuppa T l8r? C'ya'

If you're an expert text messager, don't forget that the person you're sending to might not be. Make sure they'll understand what you're talking about! Granny may have been given a mobile phone, but she may not know that 'l8r' translates as 'later', and be very confused.

A final word on how to show good manners to 'cold callers', those people who call out of the blue – usually on a Saturday morning, or just when you're sitting down to tea – to try to sell us double-glazing or a new insurance policy. They are the ones who are being rude here, and you have absolutely no obligation to listen to them. They'll usually have a 'script' that is designed to keep you on the phone as long as possible. If you're not interested, say so right away: 'Thank you. I'm not interested', and then hang up. There's no need to talk further at all, but do remember that they are mostly underpaid folk who are trying to make a living – so be firm but polite.

The letter

When was the last time you wrote a personal, handwritten letter? Communicating by letter is almost a lost art and many people hardly ever write by hand, preferring to use email, texting or the phone. It's probably ridiculous to bemoan this fact, but there are a few occasions when nothing can beat a handwritten note or letter.

Thank-you letters, for instance, can be emailed, but do look more personal and thoughtful if handwritten, perhaps on some nice paper or a card. Messages of congratulation or condolence are best sent by handwritten note, especially the latter. In general, if the message is a delicate or personal one, or one to commemorate an occasion (the birth of a child, or a wedding, or a first job), a handwritten card or letter can seem more special – and it's also something recipient can hang on to and treasure.

Business letters are another matter. They still thrive, mainly because a 'hard copy' letter provides clear evidence that something has been notified or agreed and that evidence can be kept on file. Even so, many businesses increasingly use email today – print out and keep any very important notifications if you are concerned to have copies on file. How you write a business letter is less a case of good manners than a case of the correct 'protocol'. This is because there must be no opportunity for misunderstanding. So, a formal business letter should state clearly which company it is from, what job position the writer has in that company, and the date. The address provided should be sufficient for you to contact the business if you need to, and will usually have the phone and email details too.

A business letter starts with a salutation (Dear...) and then continues with a line describing the subject of the letter, and a reference to any previous correspondence related to the subject.

Most business letters will look something like this:

> Mr James Snodgrass
> Sales Director
> Widgets International plc
> Busy Industrial Estate
> Anyroad
> Anytown
> AN3 WH6
> Tel 01222 000000
> Email: jsnodgrass@widgetint.co.uk

Your ref DBH/WJP/2376

25 February 2020

Mr D. B. Hardcase
Grummets Consolidated
Otherstreet
Othertown
TH6 TH7

Re: Giant widgets

A good business letter explains the matter concerned simply, and in plain English. If you're the one writing a business letter, don't feel that you have to use strange 'business language' or old-fashioned phrases. Just write in simple language, as you would if you were talking to someone and concentrate on keeping to the subject and explaining it clearly. There's no need to try and impress someone with 'posh' talk, and very few businesspeople would try to nowadays (with the exception of some extremely pompous lawyers, who are probably just showing off).

The important thing is to express the matter clearly and correctly. Make sure that all your sentences make sense and check the spelling and grammar, making sure that all the capital letters and full stops are in the right places. The usual kind of thing. If the letter is an important one, especially if you are in some kind of dispute with a customer, it can help to have someone else read the letter over, to make sure it does the job – a friend or colleague. If it's a legal matter, consult a solicitor, who will usually write the letter for a fee, in a way that fits any legal requirements.

Always be courteous in letters, even if you are in dispute with someone. A good business letter can be firm, and make demands, but should never be rude. Remember, if you end up getting your 'day in court', your letter may do so too – and be read out in front of everyone present.

Addressing people

While we're talking about going to court, we'll point out that this is one of the few places where there are still formal 'manners', or etiquette, defining how you should address someone – what 'form of address' you should use to speak to them.

There was a time when the top brass had to be addressed in specific ways – the folks with titles, honours and letters after their name. As already mentioned, this is really a hangover from the days of formal etiquette, when 'deference' to the higher classes was expected. That's all changed now, and many people with titles, earnt through good works or by inheritance, prefer to keep quiet about them in any case. No sensible, polite person would object if you didn't address them by their title, and used Mr or Ms instead – or even their first name, depending on the circumstances. That being said, few of us would rush over to the Queen and say 'Hi, Liz, how are you doing?'

More seriously, members of the legal profession are still referred to by their official forms of address, when they are in court. So are some senior officers in the armed forces, when they are on official business. And of course some people still prefer to be called by their title in all circumstances. If you're not sure, it's probably best to be as formal as possible first, and see how things go.

And, before you say, 'well, I'm not going to be bumping into Royalty down at the shops now, am I!', never say never. Because you never know. So, just in case you end up sitting next to someone very grand at dinner, here is a list of forms of address, showing the correct formal way to speak to people holding different positions. But don't despair, today it is highly unlikely that someone will take any offence at all if you don't refer to them by their full title, or properly. We're all human under our decorations and crowns.

The tables on pages 137–139 show how to address various notables, such as members of the peerage, clergy and judiciary, both verbally and in writing.

The Royals

A few last words about the Royal lot – if you get to meet a member of the Royal family, or want to write to them, the rules are simple, and not much more than ordinary good manners, actually.

If you want to write to the Queen, you begin 'Madam' and you are supposed to close with 'I have the honour to be, Madam, Your Majesty's humble and obedient servant'. Letters to other members of the royal family should begin with 'Sir' or 'Madam,' but it is also acceptable to start with 'Your Highness' and you can close with a simple 'Yours sincerely'.

If you actually meet members of the royal family in the flesh, men are supposed to bow from the neck and women should curtsy. But you really don't have to bother with all that – you can simply shake hands (whether you are a man or woman). Don't give a bone-crushing handshake, as the Queen has to shake hands hundreds of times and is probably fairly bruised by now! When you first address the Queen you should call her 'Your Majesty' and after that you address her as 'Ma'am' (to rhyme with 'van', not 'harm'). Male members of the royal family are initially addressed as 'Your Royal Highness' on being introduced, and as 'Sir' thereafter; female members are 'Your Royal Highness' and then 'Ma'am'. See, it's so easy you almost want to go off immediately to find a stray Princess to meet and greet!

General advice

If you are going to meet or write to people with titles and honours, one easy way to check exactly what titles and degrees they have is to go to your library, and look them up in *Who's Who* or *Debrett's Peerage and Baronetage*. These two rather dry and fearsome books will tell you everything you need to know about titles, decorations and degrees. If you are prepared to pay, you can consult these publications online. Failing that, you can phone the person's secretary, who will normally be only too pleased to give you the details you need and will no doubt think it very good manners of you to have taken the trouble to ask.

The Peerage

On an envelope:	Begin a letter:	Introduced as:	Addressed as:
The Duke of Hearts	Dear Duke of Hearts or Dear Duke	The Duke of Hearts	Your Grace or Duke
The Duchess of Hearts	Dear Duchess of Hearts	The Duchess of Hearts	Your Grace
	or Dear Duchess		or Duchess
The Marquess of Diamonds	Dear Lord Diamonds	Lord Diamonds	Lord Diamonds
The Marchioness of Diamonds	Dear Lady Diamonds	Lady Diamonds	Lady Diamonds
The Earl of Clubs	Dear Lord Clubs	Lord Clubs	Lord Clubs
The Countess of Clubs	Dear Lady Clubs	Lady Clubs	Lady Clubs
The Viscount Spades	Dear Lord Spades	Lord Spades	Lord Spades
The Viscountess Spades	Dear Lady Spades	Lady Spades	Lady Spades
Baron & wife:			
The Lord Hearts	Dear Lord Hearts	Lord Hearts	Lord Hearts
The Lady Hearts	Dear Lady Hearts	Lady Hearts	Lady Hearts
Baronet & wife:			
Sir James Diamonds Bt	Dear Sir James	Sir James Diamonds	Sir James
Lady Diamonds	Dear Lady Diamonds	Lady Diamonds	Lady Diamonds
Life peer & wife:			
The Lord Clubs	Dear Lord Clubs	Lord Clubs	Lord Clubs
The Lady Clubs	Dear Lady Clubs	Lady Clubs	Lady Clubs
Knight & wife:			
Sir David Spades	Dear Sir David	Sir David Spades	Sir David
Lady Spades	Dear Lady Spades	Lady Spades	Lady Spades

Communications

Church of England clergy

Archbishop:	All other Bishops::
The Most Reverend and Rt Hon The Archbishop	The Rt Rev the Lord Bishop of Wherever
of Canterbury/York	Dear Bishop
My Lord Archbishop	The Bishop of Wherever
The Archbishop of Canterbury/York	Bishop
Your Grace	

	Deans:
The Most Reverend the Lord Archbishop of Wherever	The Very Reverend, the Dean of Wherever
Dear Lord Archbishop or Dear Archbishop	Dear Dean
The Archbishop of Wherever	The Dean of Wherever
Archbishop	Dean

Bishop of London:	Vicars and Rectors:
The Rt Rev and Rt Hon the Lord Bishop of London	Dear Mr Whatever or Dear Father Whatever
Dear Bishop	Mr Whatever or Father Whatever
The Bishop of London	Mr Whatever or Farther Whatever
Bishop	Also you can say Vicar or Rector

Lawyers, politicians and the
medical profession

High Court Judge:	The Lord Mayor of Wherever
The Hon Mr Justice Jailem	My Lord Mayor
Dear Judge	**Mayor of a city:**
Mr Justice Jailem or Sir James Jailem	The Right Worshipful the Mayor of Wherever
Sir James	Dear Mr Mayor or Dear Madam Mayor
Circuit Court Judge:	The Mayor of Wherever
His Honour Judge Justice	Mr Mayor or Madam Mayor
Dear Sir	**Mayor of a town:**
Judge Justice	The Worshipful Mayor of Wherever
Judge Justice	Dear Mr Mayor or Dear Madam Mayor
MP:	The Mayor of Wherever
Mr James Slippery MP	Mr Mayor or Madam Mayor
Dear Mr Slippery	**Medical doctor:**
Mr James Slippery	Dr Mark Quack MD
Mr Slippery	Dear Dr Quack
Privy Councillor:	Dr or Mr (or Ms or Mrs) Quack
The Rt Hon James Evasive	Dr, Mr, Ms, Mrs Quack
Dear Mr Evasive	**Surgeon (Fellow of Royal College of Surgeons)**
Mr James Evasive	Mr (or Mrs of Ms) William Blade
Mr Evasive	Dear Mr, Mrs, Ms Blade
Lord Mayors:	Mr, Mrs, Ms Blade
The Rt Hon the Lord Mayor of Wherever	Mr, Mrs, Ms Blade
Dear Lord Mayor	

A good day at the office

At root, we all go to work to earn money to live on. Some people love their jobs, some people don't really think about them much once they get home, and some people would rather do anything else. However you feel about work, if you do go to the office each day, you'll know that there are certain 'rules' of behaviour and office-specific good manners, that help us get along with each other at work. After all, an office is quite an artificial social situation, where nobody has actually chosen the companions they spend so much time with.

The etiquette of work conversation is quite a tricky situation at times, especially when you're the new person in the office. In general, people at work tend to keep conversation light and friendly, not too personal – mostly to do with what was on TV last night, the football, general topics. Chatting is fine, but chatting about very personal matters is, in a way, not good manners, with people you only know through work. Of course, as we get to know people at work better, that can change and people from work can become close friends whom we see outside work. But, in general, it's good manners to keep away from personal matters when having work conversations, and it's certainly not good manners to spread malicious gossip about colleagues, however tempting it may seem when they're getting on your nerves.

What to wear for work? In some situations that difficult decisions is done for you, if a uniform or 'required dress' is stipulated. Some offices do have a dress code, unwritten or not, that men wear a suit and tie, and in general everyone should be smart. It is good manners to fit in, as you are representing the company's 'public face', and never know when you may be asked to meet with a client or potential customer.

Offices have other rules, both formal and informal, that it's good manners to observe. Of course some of these rules – such as when to start and end work, or when to take a coffee break – may well be fixed, and you are required to observe them as part of your job. In some offices, rules on coffee breaks etc are more relaxed, and people can choose when to get up from their work for a break. Don't abuse this flexibility – it's easy to do so inadvertently, but make sure that you put in as much work as your colleagues, and are willing to perform your job duties. People may not say anything, but they do notice the person who is 'always disappearing for a coffee' – don't let it be you!

When it comes to working hours – it's a fact of the working day that, in many jobs, people do work a little longer than their 'official' hours. Perhaps they work through lunch to get an important job done, or stay a little later to finish up something that's needed for tomorrow. Everyone chips in and, providing the employers don't abuse this willingness, it's part and parcel of the job. Take this on board, and don't be a stickler for exact time-keeping, who always rushes off home as the clock strikes 5pm.

Doing a deal

When a deal is struck, a contract is drawn up and the official procedures go into motion. But, especially in the UK and much of Europe, there is still an old custom of 'sealing the deal on a handshake' – this is technically a good-mannered way of saying 'right, we're agreed!', before doing the paperwork. There was, however, a time when a handshake really was all that was needed to strike a deal, and even though a written contract is most normal today, a handshake or verbal agreement can be considered binding in court.

But if you do 'shake hands on it', you should always send an email, fax or letter that confirms the deal and what has been agreed on. And in the case of big deals, a legal contract is vital. You may have the good manners to stand by your handshake, others may not.

Friends and lovers

For many of us the office becomes integral to our social life. Friends from work are people we also socialise with outside the office and become close pals. Usually office socialising is just that – everyone in the office, or everyone in a team or group. Every situation is different, but do think twice before striking up close friendships (platonic or otherwise) with just one or two other colleagues – it can be seen as rather cliquey and exclusive behaviour and other colleagues may feel a bit left out (or that you're a bit stuck up). Use your common sense, and be sensitive to the situation in your particular environment.

On the whole, if you're having a sexual relationship with another member of staff, the situation is likely to be problematic, especially if they are your boss (or vice versa). But many people start relationships with people they have met at work and in most offices there is no strict rule against this. Some firms, however, do frown on it, mainly because it can cause problems in the workplace, and is seen as damaging to the company's efficiency. If a couple break up, it can – as you can imagine – make for a bit of tension in the air. If possible, it's probably best for one of you to find a job at a different company, or in a different department, though of course you may not have that opportunity. It's good manners not to 'canoodle' all over the place in front of work colleagues: behave in a normal and professional manner to all office colleagues, including your partner.

But, on the whole, general office socialising isn't problematic for most companies – in fact it can be a great bonding exercise to have a regular Friday night out at the pub, or a party when some big work project is completed on time.

Hierarchy

Once you settle into a new job you get a much clearer idea of the hierarchy. Obvious information, like someone's job title or description, their office size and, if you know it, their salary, will give you a safe indication of where that person fits in, in relation to you.

Office politics can require good manners in situations when we'd, to be honest, rather be a bit rude! For instance, it's in our own interest to show respect and good manners to our boss or supervisor. After all, to put it bluntly, they may be the person deciding our next promotion or pay rise. If you happen to find your boss a bit aggravating, try not to show it – show them how competent and willing you are, instead.

Remember, even though you may well be on first-name terms with everyone in your office, there is still an unwritten hierarchy, based on job position. That's not to say that bosses are in any way allowed to bully, threaten or otherwise harass other people in the office, but they do – to be realistic – have a bit more power.

If you're looking to move up the ladder at work, get to know where everyone sits in the hierarchy. An easy way to do this is to pay attention at meetings, and be sure you know who does what, and who's 'in' with who. Many offices have a great many meetings – some people say that they have so many meetings at work they don't have time to get any work done! To be cynical, you can get a lot of work done in a meeting, just learning about the office hierarchy.

Passing the buck

Quite often, people are worried about their job security, or anxious to be seen as good at their job. A lot of 'buck passing' can go on in business, done by people who don't want to get the blame when things go wrong and are quite happy to blame it on someone else – or at least imply someone else was the cause of the problem. Don't be a buck-passer: it's one of the most ill-mannered office behaviours going. Nobody will respect you, and even if you think nobody knows, your colleagues are probably onto your *modus operandi* already.

If someone 'passes the buck' to you, there's sadly little you can do about it without appearing to be whining. But there are ways that you can firmly and calmly assert 'actually Jim, Eric was in charge of the Burton's account, and he prepared that report' if there is a factual actuality that you can point to. Otherwise, be assured that most bosses are well aware of who the habitual buck-passers are, and try to shake it off.

Customers and clients: the outside world

Do you work in a situation where you have to meet people from 'outside'? Most people have to be in contact with people from outside the company at some point in their work, even if it's just someone passing through to have a look at the workshop, or visit the factory. And, in an office or a business that provides a service, it may well be part of your job to deal with the general public.

Put yourself in the customer's position for a moment. They are hoping to be met by someone who's clean, tidy, and interested to help them. If you are still wearing that filthy shirt from Monday, haven't shaved, and just grunt at them when they ring the bell on the counter, you're not really going to win the 'employee of the month badge'! But worst of all is being rude, offhand, or simply bored – even if you are very busy, the customer always comes first. That very old adage still stands. And most of all, be informed – the customer needs information from you. If you don't know the answer to a question, find out who does.

But that doesn't mean you have to grovel, and no customer has the right to treat anyone like some kind of servant or slave. So, if you're on the customer side of this equation, remember that you're approaching an equal, and be polite – even if you have come in to complain about something.

If you are introduced to a visiting client at work, simply smile, stand if appropriate, and offer your hand to shake. You don't have to be a conversational genius; you can just say something friendly and polite like 'hello, how are you today?' or 'nice to meet you, how was your journey?'. Most importantly, if a visitor appears in your office and is hanging around looking lost, don't ignore them. There's nothing more embarrassing than being left to wait, without knowing who to approach. If there is nobody to greet them, then you should be on your feet and walking towards them, with a smile and a 'hello, you look a bit lost – can I help you?' or something similarly friendly. If

If you are introduced to a visiting client at work, simply smile, stand if appropriate, and offer your hand to shake.

you really have to finish some work first, smile and say 'I'll be with you in just a moment, do sit down' or something like that. Or, if you just can't leave your work, ask a colleague to do the honours.

Do remember that older visitors just may not be used to informality. They may not sit down until offered a chair. Always try to imagine how the other person is thinking.

If a supplier visits your office, the situation is rather different. They are there to sell you something and will be trying to make a good impression. If you are a supplier's rep, you'll know that a polite, friendly and presentable manner will get you a long way.

There's just no point in turning up looking scruffy and dirty, or being late. People won't take you seriously, however good the product you're selling. So, even if you spend most of your time oiling motorcycle gaskets, when you go out on the road to sell those gaskets, put on a clean outfit, smarten up a bit, and practice a few smiles and firm handshakes.

If you're expecting a supplier, be courteous and don't keep them waiting. They may have several offices or businesses to visit that day. It pays to treat everyone courteously, because, for a start, you never know when the tables might be turned and it's you that's waiting for an appointment to sell your wares!

Cross words and confrontations

Perhaps it just can't be helped: it's inevitable that sometimes complaints are necessary and sometimes arguments break out. If you can't avoid an argument, at least play by these simple rules of good manners:

- If it really isn't the person's fault, don't stand there shouting at them. A shop assistant probably has no say in the shop's 'returns' policy, for instance, so you shouldn't take it out on him or her. Shouting won't get you anywhere. Asking for the address of head office and writing a letter of complaint about the policy may, especially if you explain just why you are so cross about it – in firm, but courteous language.

- Even if you have got the 'right' person, what's the point of shouting? There's no excuse for abuse and besides, it just won't help the situation. Of course, we've all given into our anger now and then, but we shouldn't. For a start, you'll upset everyone in the vicinity – not just the person you're aiming at. Stick to the facts, be firm and by all means cross, but in a civil and measured way. Present the facts, be calm and polite, but refuse to be fobbed off. Keep going as long as you have the power to do so in the hope that you will eventually persuade them to help you.

- If you're going to write a letter of complaint, do it with care. Anything you write will leave a permanent record and it can be read by anyone – even presented in court. So bear this in mind and think about how your words will sound to the person reading it. If you sound too angry and aggressive, tone it down – this doesn't mean you have to leave out any facts, or that you have to 'give in'. Simply be firm and demand action. A successful letter of complaint is one directed to the right person (if in doubt, call the company or shop and ask), and one that not only complains but asks for a practical solution. Writing to the head of a company can help too: the chairman of Marks and Spencer may not personally read the letter of complaint you wrote him about the overly small sandwiches, but he'll probably pass it on to someone who will – because your custom is needed.

- Finally, be magnanimous in victory and stoical in defeat. This means that if you get what you wanted from the situation, don't rub your opponent's nose in it. Simply accept graciously. And if you don't succeed, just accept it on the chin and face the fact that you did your best. No point in going on further.

Index